Teach® urself

Be Your Own Personality Coach

Paul Jenner

Hodder Education

338 Euston Road, London NW1 3BH.

Hodder Education is an Hachette UK company

First published in UK 2011 by Hodder Education

First published in US 2011 by The McGraw-Hill Companies, Inc.

This edition published 2011.

www.hoddereducation.co.uk

Typeset by Cenveo Publisher Services.

Printed in Great Britain by CPI Cox & Wyman, Reading.

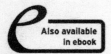

Also available in ebook

This book is dedicated to Bethany, Annabella and Elodie whose different personalities are a great delight.

Acknowledgements

A very special thank you to Victoria Roddam, my publisher at Hodder Education.

Image credits

Contents

Meet the author

What is it to have a successful personality? Automatically, we tend to think of the kind of people who excel on game shows. We think ambition, sociability, warmth, optimism, energy and so on.

But, in fact, every personality has its disadvantages as well as its advantages. That extrovert, so popular on the game show, may be quite inept in other kinds of situations.

What it really means to be successful is to know and understand the characteristic pattern of thoughts, feelings and behaviours that comprise your personality and to direct them at suitable targets.

This book will coach you in four areas. The first is measuring personality, so you can know yourself, and others, better. The second is learning how to exploit your personality most successfully to achieve your major life goals, including love, happiness and wealth. The third is understanding why you are the way you are. And finally the book will explain techniques for modifying your personality, *if you wish*.

You're about to embark on a fascinating expedition to map the real you. I think some of your discoveries will surprise you. And you're certainly going to have fun. Enjoy it.

Paul Jenner (Spain, 2011)

In one minute

Your complete personality (the characteristic pattern of your thoughts, feelings and behaviours) can be captured in terms of just five traits. The 'Big Five' are Openness, Conscientiousness, Extroversion, Agreeableness and Neuroticism (remembered by the acronym OCEAN).

Your gender is liable to have a significant impact on your personality, from empathy to your risk appetite.

The face is a very poor guide to personality but choosing a similar face to your own is a proven tactic for romantic success.

The most faithful partners are likely to be those high in Conscientiousness and Agreeableness and low in Extroversion and Openness.

Phrenology, the Rorschach ink blot test, birth order, handwriting and star signs are all 'personality poppycock'.

High Conscientiousness is associated with higher lifetime earnings, while high Agreeableness in couples is associated with lower earnings.

You can increase your creativity (higher Openness) by exercising the right hemisphere of your brain.

Most human beings have a strong urge to conform and to obey authority.

Increased happiness results from a conscious decision to pursue both external sources and internal resources.

Your unconscious mind is responsible for running a huge part of your life…and maybe all of it.

Letting chance into your life increases the possibility of discovering the real you.

High Neuroticism can be tackled using cognitive therapy.

NLP can increase your scores for Openness, Conscientiousness, Extroversion and Agreeableness.

1

··

The Big Five

In this chapter you will learn:
- *how to measure personality*
- *the Big Five personality traits*
- *your own five-factor personality scores.*

Most psychologists now agree that your personality, and everyone
else's, can usefully be defined in terms of just five traits. According to
this five-factor model, you are the product of various amounts of:

▶ Openness
▶ Conscientiousness
▶ Extroversion
▶ Agreeableness
▶ Neuroticism.

I've stated them in that order because they can then easily be
remembered using the acronym OCEAN, but there's no particular
order of importance. Of course, you may wish to argue that your
personality is far too complex to be reduced to a web of five
dimensions. Raymond Catell (1905–1998), one of the outstanding
psychologists of his time, used a framework of 16 traits and the most
recent edition of the test that he first introduced in 1949 has as many
as 185 multiple-choice questions. His 16 factors are:

▶ warmth
▶ reasoning
▶ emotional stability
▶ dominance

▶ liveliness
▶ rule-consciousness
▶ social boldness
▶ sensitivity

- ▶ vigilance
- ▶ abstractedness
- ▶ privateness
- ▶ apprehension
- ▶ openness to change
- ▶ self-reliance
- ▶ perfectionism
- ▶ tension.

But, in fact, Catell, too, considered that there were five 'global' or 'second-order' factors that are more or less the Big Five.

At the opposite end of the scale, the specialist in personality theory Hans Eysenck (1916–1997) concluded that no matter how 'deep' you think you are, it's possible to capture your personality with just two factors, Extroversion and Neuroticism. Variations in these two provided four basic personality types (very much as the Greek physician Hippocrates had proposed more than 2,000 years earlier). But in the 1970s Eysenck added a third factor to his model, Psychoticism, which largely corresponded with the traits of Agreeableness and Conscientiousness.

So he, too, came close to the Big Five, and that's where the consensus is now.

....

Insight

In this context, a Big Five trait is a bundle of characteristics that normally come together, so that if you have one characteristic in the bundle you'll have the others, too. Nobody can say any particular number of traits is right or wrong. There are different ways of measuring personality, just as you can measure a box in centimetres or in inches. The method doesn't change the box. The beauty of the Big Five is simply that it's a system on which large numbers of psychologists all over the world have agreed. It makes it easier to carry out research and to standardize therapies. It also means you can now compare yourself with people from the UK to the USA, and from Uruguay to Uzbekistan.

....

In a moment I'm going to give you the opportunity to build a comprehensive picture of your personality by answering a mere 20 questions. But first, let's get an idea of what these Big Five traits mean. Each of them is a continuum on which you will score somewhere between low and high.

So let's see where you lie along each of these scales and what that implies in terms of your personality.

Trait	If you score low, you will be	If you score high you, will be
Openness	Conventional	Creative, artistic, eccentric
Conscientiousness	Careless, impulsive	Organized, self-disciplined
Extroversion	Quiet, withdrawn	Expansive, enthusiastic
Agreeableness	Uncooperative, unfriendly	Empathetic, sociable
Neuroticism	Stable, confident	Anxious, stressed

The quick Big Five test

Simply rate the extent to which each of the following statements is an accurate description of you:

	Inaccurate			Accurate	
	Very	Moderately	Neither	Moderately	Very
Group 1					
Have a rich vocabulary					
Easily understand abstract ideas					
Have a vivid imagination					
Like to be creative					
Group 2					
Am always prepared					
Never leave my belongings around					
Pay attention to details					
Never make a mess of things					

	Very	Moderately	Neither	Moderately	Very
Group 3					
Am the life of the party					
Talk a lot					
Feel comfortable around people					
Keep in the foreground					
Group 4					
Feel concern for others					
Am interested in people					
Never insult people					
Sympathize with others' feelings					
Group 5					
Get stressed out easily					
Seldom feel relaxed					
Worry about things					
Often feel blue					

Scoring

For every 'very inaccurate' score 1.

For every 'moderately inaccurate' score 2.

For every 'neither' score 3.

For every 'moderately accurate' score 4.

For every 'very accurate' score 5.

(This is a short version of the International Personality Item Pool (IPIP), adapted by me. If you would like to take a more detailed 50 or 100 item questionnaire you will find it online at http://ipip.ori.org.)

So in any Group you could score anything from a low of 4 up to a high of 20, with a median of 12. Now let's take a look at what your scores mean.

Group 1 – Openness

Group 1 measures the personality dimension that, at its highest, is associated with creative people such as poets, artists and composers. Some psychologists use the term 'Intellect' and some 'Culture' but the most common tag is 'Openness to experience' or just 'Openness'.

If you scored high on Openness, you almost certainly enjoy not just some but more or less all cultural activities such as going to concerts, plays and art galleries, and probably are very creative yourself, either professionally or in an amateur way. You're probably unconventional and individualistic; other people may consider you eccentric. You may ignore or oppose taboos and you'll probably have more lifetime sexual partners than average. You probably spent longer in education than the norm and, according to some psychologists, Openness is a reflection of greater efficiency in the cognitive circuits in the frontal lobes of the brain. In other words, you should be of above average intelligence.

Your Openness also probably extends to what are known as 'unusual experiences', which means you're likely to experience hallucinations or something close to them, to believe in the supernatural, to have unusual religious beliefs, to be susceptible to hypnosis, and to use language and images in unusual ways. At the most extreme all of this may add up to psychosis, that's to say, being out of touch with reality.

Self-coaching tip

It's important to understand that there's no 'right' or 'wrong' amount of Openness or of any of the other Big Five traits. Each point on the continuum has its advantages and disadvantages. But if you want to change your degree of Openness, then you probably want to increase it (while falling short of psychosis) and we'll be looking at how to do that later in the book.

Group 2 – Conscientiousness

Group 2 measures Conscientiousness which, in this context, means self-discipline and self-control. If you're very low in Conscientiousness, you may find it hard to focus on one thing for any length of time and as a child you may have been diagnosed with attention-deficit hyperactivity disorder (ADHD). If you were, you're probably male because the condition occurs five times more often among boys than girls. As a person low in Conscientiousness, you'll also be highly impulsive and prone to become addicted to whatever gives you a buzz, such as adrenaline sports, gambling, alcohol, and drugs.

At the other end of the scale, if you're high in Conscientiousness you may get the same buzz but you'll easily be capable of controlling it.

In tests of people's ability to inhibit their responses to stimuli, those who were the most successful (the most Conscientiousness) showed considerable activity in the dorsolateral prefrontal and orbit ofrontal brain areas. Those who were the least successful (the most impulsive) had far lower activity in these areas.

As someone high in Conscientiousness, you'll be good at making plans and sticking to them, at paying attention to details, and at dealing with repetitive tasks. At its upper extreme, Conscientiousness becomes obsessive-compulsive personality disorder. (Note that OCPD is not the same as obsessive-compulsive disorder, in which sufferers feel compelled to repeat certain thoughts and actions such as hand-washing.) In OCPD, sufferers don't necessarily feel any need to repeat things, but are obsessed with doing things in a very precise and particular way. An OCPD sufferer might always get up at exactly the same time, eat exactly the same thing for breakfast, insist on everything being in exactly the 'right' place on the desk at work, apply rules to the letter, pursue perfection and become irritable and even disorientated if there's any deviation from the routine.

Self-coaching tip

Not surprisingly, those with high Conscientiousness tend to be the most successful in more conventional careers. But, interestingly, the most Conscientious people are not necessarily the most intelligent. In fact, the cleverer anyone is, the less Conscientious they're likely to be. That's because they can 'get away with' more. Conscientiousness can be a way of making up for being less bright (which is another way of saying that genius is 90 per cent perspiration and only 10 per cent inspiration). If you're not very high in Conscientiousness, it helps to be clever. Or you need to seek occupations that generate enough excitement to maintain your interest – but make sure someone else is paying attention to the details (especially to do with safety).

Group 3 – Extroversion

Group 3 measures the extent to which anybody prefers action to reflection, and company to solitude, that's to say, Extroversion. It was the Swiss psychiatrist Carl Jung (1875–1961) who first developed the idea of the extroverted and introverted personalities. The Big Five trait of Extroversion with a capital E explores very much the same continuum but is not quite the same.

If you scored high in Extroversion, you're talkative and like social occasions at which you aim to be the centre of attention. You're open to new friendships but they don't necessarily go well. You're probably ambitious and crave status, so you work hard but also play hard, enjoying travel, adventurous activities and new sensations. You're also likely to enjoy sex and romance more than average.

Given all the attributes associated with scoring high on the scale of Extroversion, who would wish to be low (that is, Introverted) if they could possibly help it? Apart from anything else, a low score is associated with *anhedonia*, which means deriving less pleasure from things than other people (or no pleasure at all). But Introversion is not without its own rewards. Let's say that things are simply enjoyed in a quieter, more measured way. Nor is the commonly held belief that Introverts are shy necessarily correct. Shyness is related to high Neuroticism, not low Extroversion. If you're an introvert, it may just be that you don't derive as much pleasure from social events and parties as you do from, say, reading. The introvert is not the puppet of either unconditioned (natural) stimuli, such as food, nor of conditioned stimuli, such as luxury brands, but is more in control of life.

Insight

Although Extroverts respond powerfully to positive things, they don't have a similarly powerful response to negative things. It's entirely a matter of reactivity to rewarding stimuli. Magnetic Resonance Imaging has shown that when a reward is anticipated, the regions of the brain known as the nucleus accumbens and the ventral tegmental area become more active. These regions contain neurons that respond to the neurotransmitter dopamine. It seems that Extroverts are highly responsive to dopamine, while those low in Extroversion are less responsive.

Self-coaching tip

Although high Extroversion may sound attractive, it doesn't come without risks. Research suggests that Extroverts die younger, almost certainly because they're more likely to engage in risky activities such as drinking, smoking, driving fast, and going places others don't dare. So if you're high in Extroversion you may want to rein yourself in a bit.

Group 4 – Agreeableness

Group 4 measures how considerate, empathetic, trusting and co-operative you are, a group of qualities coming under the heading Agreeableness. It also measures to what extent you have what psychologists call a 'theory of mind'. It's a rather confusing term because it doesn't mean what most people would think. If you have a highly developed 'theory of mind', it means you have the ability to guess fairly accurately what other people are thinking and, in addition, to understand what other people are feeling and, to some degree, to feel it, too. So theory of mind comes in two parts, 'mentalizing' and 'empathizing'.

It's possible to be good at one but not the other. Psychopaths, for example, can be good at working out how other people will think, but without feeling any concern for the anguish and pain they may inflict on them. Autistic individuals are the reverse. They struggle to understand what other people are thinking, but when they see clear physical evidence that someone is suffering in some way they can respond sympathetically.

A theory of mind has already developed to some extent by the age of 18 months. Such toddlers do not imitate indiscriminately. For example, if an adult tries to do something and fails (or pretends to fail), an 18-month-old will copy what the adult tried to do, not what he or she actually did do. Nevertheless, the theory of mind is not *fully* developed until about the age of four. That's why an infant can put a box over their head and imagine that they have become invisible. Because they can't see, they believe that no one else can see.

This has been demonstrated a little more scientifically using a puppet show known as Sally-Anne. Two puppets, Sally and Anne, play with a ball. Sally then places the ball in a basket and leaves the room. Anne takes the ball out of the basket and hides it in a box. Sally returns. The children are then asked: Where will Sally look for the ball?

Children under four think Sally will look in the box. They know the ball is in the box and assume Sally must know it, too. It's only after the age of four, approximately, that children understand that Sally will still expect the ball to be in the basket.

This becomes less surprising when we realize that other animals, even the highest, don't have a very developed theory of mind, if at all. Chimpanzees, for example, give a rather disappointing account of themselves in an experiment that almost all humans 'pass' easily. Two chimps (or humans) sit facing one another. Chimp A has access to two levers. Pulling the first lever brings chimp A some tasty food. Pulling the second lever not only brings chimp A the same food, but also produces food for chimp B. So what happens?

Almost all humans pull the second lever. It's what we've come to call a 'win-win situation'. Why wouldn't you pull it? It costs you nothing and another person also benefits. But chimps don't think like that, even if the other chimp is a relative. Their only concern is their own meal.

So chimps and, it seems, most non-human animals are pretty low on empathy. But that doesn't mean they're no good at the other aspect of theory of mind, that is, the mentalizing. Assessing the mentalizing ability of animals is no easy thing but I've many times seen behaviours that convince me it's more highly developed than many scientists allow. I've seen ponies hiding from one another and I've seen them deliberately galloping off when an unpopular pony was busy with its head down. Scientists tell me horses don't have the ability to play practical jokes. They point to Nim Chimpsky, one of the world's most educated chimps, who would copy the way a human companion washed dishes but never actually cleaned them. Nim could emulate the movements but didn't understand – couldn't mentalize – *why* someone was doing it.

Nevertheless, I continue to believe that the mentalizing abilities of animals are underrated. Assessing the mentalizing abilities of humans is somewhat easier. In one set of experiments, participants were asked to listen to stories and then say whether or not certain statements about the beliefs of the characters in the stories were true or not. Sounds easy enough. But the questions required a fairly complex ability called 'nesting'. If you're good at nesting, you can not only understand someone else's beliefs, but you can also understand their beliefs about someone else's beliefs...about someone else's beliefs...and so on. Some people (those with lots of friends) are generally very much better at it than others (those with few friends). See if you can keep track of this:

▶ Peter thought that Charlene thought Esther believed that Sam wanted to go on holiday with Mark because Sam thought Esther wanted to go on holiday alone.

So that's clear, then.

The advantages of being low on Agreeableness seem compelling in evolutionary terms. You can ruthlessly exploit others to your own advantage. But is it really true that nice guys finish last? Actually, it's not, neither in evolutionary terms nor in terms of human society today. Co-operation can be a much better strategy, as a game known as the Prisoner's Dilemma illustrates. Here it is.

THE PRISONER'S DILEMMA

You and the other player each have two cards, one labelled 'Co-operate' and the other 'Defect'. You each make your choice and place your card face down on the table (to be turned over after you've both played). That means there are four possible outcomes. For each outcome a banker would pay out as follows:

- ▶ You both played 'Co-operate'. You each win 300 units (pounds, dollars, ounces of gold or whatever).
- ▶ You both played 'Defect'. You are each fined 10 units.
- ▶ You played 'Co-operate', the other person played 'Defect'. You are fined 100 units; the other person wins 500 units.
- ▶ You played 'Defect', the other person played 'Co-operate'. You win 500 units; the other person is fined 100 units.

What would you do? What *should* you do? It's more than an entertaining puzzle because in life there are many situations in which it's necessary to choose between co-operating or not.

Well, if your opponent has played 'Defect', the best you can do is also play 'Defect', which incurs a fine of 10 units (if you played 'Co-operate' the fine would be 100 units). But if your opponent has played 'Co-operate', the best you can do is play 'Defect', which wins 500 units (as opposed to 300 units if you also played Co-operate). So the best strategy for a *single* game is that you play 'Defect'.

But supposing you play the game repeatedly, which is how things tend to be in real life? In that case, you have the opportunity to feel out your opponent, which changes things a bit. Obviously, you'd win the most money if you always played 'Defect' and the other person always played 'Co-operate', but that would never actually happen because of the fine of 100 units. Being realistic, it turns out that the best strategy is 'Tit for Tat'. You play 'Co-operate' on the first hand and on subsequent hands you simply copy whatever your opponent did on the previous hand. Don't just take my word for it – it's been tested on computer models. (You can read more about it in Chapter 8.)

Group 5 – Neuroticism

Group 5, measures how worried, upset, ashamed, guilty, sad or frightened you become in response to a negative stimulus, that's to say, Neuroticism.

If you've ever ridden a horse, you'll know it's an animal that could very well be labelled Neurotic. It flees, or tries to, at the merest hint of possible trouble. A strangely shaped piece of wood, a white boulder, leaves moving in the wind, something that's not where it used to be... These are all things to which horses can respond very dramatically. Horses are prey animals. It was high Neuroticism that kept the species going. Unfortunately, even though most horses today have never seen a predator capable of bringing them down, they can't easily overcome the response that evolution has programmed into them. Humans, too, could be prey at one time. Now we're the top predators on the planet. But many humans, like horses, struggle to control their Neuroticism.

At its extreme, high Neuroticism is associated with a whole range of problems including insomnia, phobias, eating disorders, post-traumatic stress disorders, depression and obsessive compulsive disorder or OCD. (Remember that OCD is not the same thing as obsessive-compulsive personality disorder, which was discussed in connection with Conscientiousness above.)

The really devastating aspect to very high Neuroticism is that it becomes a self-fulfilling prophecy. Although the majority of worries never materialize, Neurotics nevertheless tend to suffer more negative life events than other people. They tend to have more health problems brought on by stress (which depresses the immune system), depression and insomnia. They tend to have more life problems because they're difficult to live with. They may have career problems because they suffer low self-esteem.

Are there no benefits to high Neuroticism? Well, yes. Although Neurotics tend to have more health problems, they seem to suffer fewer accidents because they take fewer risks. They tend to be more realistic, which probably makes them more dependable in many aspects of life. And because they're always worried about failing and losing their jobs, they tend to work harder.

Self-coaching tip

So, assuming it was within your power, where on the scale of Neuroticism would you want to be in order to be successful? Given that the majority of the things we all worry about never actually happen (or are far less terrible than we imagined), high Neuroticism wastes a lot of time and energy. Of all the Big Five, it's possible to argue that Neuroticism is the trait for which you'd like to score the lowest. But remember that high Neuroticism also has its career advantages. Paradoxically, if you're very Neurotic, you could do well wherever potentially high-risks need to be reduced.

Is there any point in personality tests?

Although the Big Five model has become widely adopted, it's not without its problems. There's an apparent contradiction at the very heart of the Openness trait, for example. It's this: people who score high in Openness also score high in terms of Unusual Experiences and in IQ tests. But when people who score high for Unusual Experiences are given IQ tests, their scores are *lower* than average. This is something psychologists are still arguing about.

As regards the Extroversion continuum, Eysenck proposed that introverts actually have naturally *higher* levels of cortical arousal than Extroverts, rather than lower levels, as many suppose. As a result, they don't seek out the 'artificial' arousal that extroverts require to feel 'normal'. Another problem with the theory of Extroversion is that it takes no account of *motive*. Introverts may be highly sexed with *one* person, for example, and they can and do take part in adventure sports, but they may do so in pursuit of spiritual experiences or solitude rather than an adrenaline rush. (Not surprisingly, though, those who take part in adventure sports are almost always low in Neuroticism.)

Criticisms are not confined to Big Five tests. The Myers-Briggs Type Indicator, long the most widely used system among employers, has been attacked for being too rooted in Swiss psychologist Carl Jung's book *Psychological Types*. Developed by Isabel Briggs Myers and her mother Katharine Cook Briggs (and now belonging to Consulting Psychologists Press Inc.), the Myers-Briggs uses four basic traits: extroversion/introversion, sensate/intuitive, thinking/feeling and judging/perceiving. There are therefore 16 broad personality types possible, each indicated by a four-letter code. For example, ENFP stands for extroversion, intuitive, feeling, perceiving. But Jung (1875–1961) was a man who worked very much from his clinical experience and from anecdotes and who had a strong distrust for statistical methods. Later in the book, we'll see why he should have paid more attention to the discipline.

But there's a much wider criticism of these kinds of personality tests. Of course, we all like to do them. If we come across a personality test in a magazine, we're drawn to it as if by a magnet. We tick the boxes, add up the points and enjoy reading how wonderful we are. But no matter how serious the tests, they only tell us *what we already know*.

In the quick version of the Big Five test above, for example, did you agree that 'Like to be creative' was a very accurate description of yourself? And, if you did, were you astonished to discover that you are, indeed, creative? Or if you indicated that 'Am the life of the party' was a very inaccurate description, were you surprised to be defined as low in Extroversion?

Of course, personality tests are not just undertaken for the entertainment and education of the subjects themselves. Increasingly, nowadays, employers will ask you to take such tests. There you are, applying for a job at the bank, and you mark that 'Pay attention to details' is a very inaccurate description of your personality... I think not! Those who design personality tests for employers may make theirs rather less transparent, but it's not easy to disguise entirely the answers that stand the best chance of getting the job.

Then there are people who consult psychologists because they have problems. You would assume, in pursuit of being helped, that anyone in that situation would complete a questionnaire as accurately as possible. But, for a variety of reasons, people with psychological problems may be unwilling or incapable of being honest.

To overcome these drawbacks, there is a whole different style known as projective testing. We'll be meeting that later in Chapter 4.

10 TIPS FOR SUCCESS

1 Just five traits are commonly used to describe personality.

2 The five traits are Openness, Conscientiousness, Extroversion, Agreeableness and Neuroticism (remembered by the acronym OCEAN).

3 A trait is a bundle of characteristics that normally come together.

4 Other famous systems use from 2 to 16 factors.

5 If you score high in Openness, you're unconventional and creative.

6 If you score high in Conscientiousness, you pay attention to details and are good at controlling impulses.

7 If you're high in Extroversion, you respond powerfully to pleasurable stimuli.

8 If you're high in Agreeableness, you understand what other people are thinking and readily empathize.

9 If you're high in Neuroticism, you quickly feel negative emotions such as anxiety, fear and guilt.

10 The value of personality tests is debatable.

2

The Big *One*

In this chapter you will learn:
- *how evolution shaped men's and women's personalities differently*
- *why gender differences are natural*
- *why women are choosy and men aren't.*

I'm now going to tell you how you can understand a huge amount about someone's personality by knowing not 16 traits, nor five, nor even two, but merely a single fact. This technique is so powerful I call it The Big *One*. I warn you that some people get very annoyed when I insist on the importance of The Big *One*, but there's plenty of scientific evidence for a powerful influence on:

- ▶ how empathetic you are
- ▶ how emotional you are
- ▶ how good you are with language
- ▶ how conciliatory you are
- ▶ how sensitive you are to sounds and smells
- ▶ how often you laugh
- ▶ how competitive you are
- ▶ how violent you are
- ▶ how easily you can manipulate three-dimensional objects in your mind
- ▶ how likely you are to have some kind of learning disability
- ▶ how much pain you can tolerate
- ▶ how likely you are to take risks
- ▶ how much time you spend thinking about sex
- ▶ how easily aroused you are by an attractive naked body
- ▶ how likely you are to engage in one-night stands
- ▶ how likely you are to be above average height for a human being.

Yes, you've guessed it. The Big *One* is gender. If you're a woman, you're likely to be at the higher end of the scale for the first six and at the lower end for all the rest. If you're a man, the reverse is likely to be the case.

Your gender is one of the biggest influences on your personality. *Some* women may be just as violent, just as risk-taking and just as open to one-night stands as *some* men. But taken as a whole, men and women *are* different. Why they're different is controversial. Some feminists have argued that it's all a matter of cultural influences. But the weight of science is on evolution. Sexual differences exist in the physical structure of the brain and much of that difference exists *before* birth, as we'll discover in Chapter 10.

Let's start with a sperm and an egg. Why are they so very different? Why is an egg so big (relatively speaking) and a sperm so tiny? Why don't both parents just contribute equal cells? Part of the answer is that if both cells contained mitochondria, the 'machinery' that powers a cell, then the result would be mutual destruction. So only one of the cells – the mother's egg – contains mitochondria. A sperm cell doesn't and can therefore be much smaller.

There is another line of thinking. Let's say that in the very distant past gametes (sex cells) were all roughly the same size. Nevertheless, some might have been slightly larger than others for various reasons and those larger gametes would have conferred an advantage by reason of the more generous food supply they contained. As a result of that advantage, there would then have been a trend towards larger gametes. But that in turn would have opened up the possibility for these larger gametes to fuse successfully with much smaller ones, since the combined food supply would still have been adequate. A successful strategy would then have been organisms producing large gametes (eggs) mating with organisms that exploited the new situation by producing generous quantities of small, highly mobile gametes (sperm) that could seek out eggs more quickly.

Insight

Evidence that this was so lies in the fact that this size difference in gametes is universal. In all plants and animals, one kind produces large sex cells (and is called female) and the other kind produces small sex cells (and is called male). In fact, this is the *only* way of distinguishing males from females in *all* plants and animals (not every male animal, for example, has a penis).

Gender and personality

You may be wondering what all this stuff about the size of gametes has to do with personality. The answer is: just about everything. It's from this that all else follows.

We now have one version of a particular organism producing valuable, nutritious eggs, containing their mitochondria power stations. And we have another version specialized for producing simple sperm in large quantities. The strategies these two versions need to follow for breeding success are not identical, albeit they are members of the same species.

Let's just remind ourselves how natural selection works. Any strategy that increases reproductive success will be selected (since the genes for that strategy will become more widespread). Equally, any strategy that reduces reproductive success is automatically self-destructive and will be deselected. A male who contentedly remains with the female he fertilized gives his offspring a good chance of survival. But the male who spreads his generous supply of sperm far and wide by having sex with numerous females has numerous offspring. True, there is a trade-off. Since he cannot be a good parent to all these children, the survival rate may be lower. But, on balance, the genes of the promiscuous father are likely to be more successful than those of the faithful father.

The psychologist David Buss asked 10,000 men and women, living in all kinds of cultures in 37 countries all over the world, to rate the importance of 18 qualities in a partner. In almost every country, men attached more importance to youth and beauty than women did, and women attached more importance to wealth, status and prospects than men did.

This is exactly as would be expected in terms of evolution (and not what you would expect if everything was down to culture). Women have to make a big investment in their offspring. They carry them for nine months and look after them for years. They need to know that the father is going to stay around to help and that he will be a good provider. And since they can have relatively few children, women also need to know that those children will be healthy and successful and go on to breed in their turn. This makes women very choosy.

A man's strategy is different. Since he can theoretically father a child every day, he doesn't need to be choosy at all. His breeding strategy is to have sex with as many women as possible, 'wasting' the minimum amount of time on each.

Insight

Of course, men and women don't actually think in these terms. They may not want any children at all. But their personalities are nevertheless driven by their genes, and their genes are intent on survival – some have already survived for millions of years. All living things, humans included, are effectively just 'machines' built by genes for the benefit of genes.

Why men like pornography and women don't

We can now see why women are not very interested in pornography but men are. Men created pornography on the walls of caves thousands of years ago. A man is so easily aroused that a mere charcoal outline is enough to do the trick. Just think about it. A man can have an erection even though he knows perfectly well he's only looking at some dots of ink on a piece of paper or some coloured pixels on a computer screen.

If a woman were that easily aroused, she'd be made pregnant by the first man who came along. To men's astonishment, women don't actually think about sex very much at all. In fact, they have half the brain volume devoted to sex that men do. The now famous figure from one study is that 85 per cent of men aged between 20 and 30 think about sex every 52 seconds. The figure is rather suspect because if you ask someone to think about how often they think about something, they're bound to think about it more. Nevertheless, the same study found that women think about sex only once a day (but three to four times a day when ovulating). How often they'd think about sex if they weren't taking part in a study is something we'll never know. Whatever the true figures in 'real life', it seems pretty clear that women think about sex a lot, lot less than men do.

A woman's strategy, in evolutionary terms, requires that she not be aroused by a naked stranger, instead making a judgement based on a man's ability and willingness to provide for herself and her children. How can she do that? One way is to make men wait for sex. Those who lose interest and seek sex elsewhere demonstrate their lack of seriousness. Those who hang around prove they have at least one of the qualities necessary for successful parenting. This is the female equivalent of the man's 'bad girls for sex, nice girls for marriage' strategy. And, in fact, research into female behaviour proves that it happens in the real world. Women tend to make prospective husbands wait longer for sex than they do men they know are only going to be 'one-night stands'. In the age of effective contraception, women have flings with square-jawed macho types, but marry men with the slightly more feminine qualities that are desirable in a long-term partner and father.

When it comes to affairs after marriage, women (as would be expected) are more faithful. Statistics on this are bound to be unreliable but it seems probable that one-third to one-half of American men have at least one affair during the course of a marriage, compared with between one-fifth and two-fifths of women. Once again, a woman's greater 'investment' in a family dictates behaviour.

Insight

Most mammals are polygamous (about 97 per cent) so the scale of these figures shouldn't be surprising. Here's an intriguing thing. You can tell how polygamous a species is by comparing the size of males and females. The bigger the males, relatively speaking, the more polygamous. Successful gorillas, for example, have harems of three to six females, and are roughly double their size. Gibbons, on the other hand, are monogamous and the sexes are almost the same size. Why? Because the more polygamous a species is, the more the males have to fight over the females, and the more size becomes an advantage.

What about humans? The intriguing thing is that men used to be about 50 per cent larger than women in the early Middle Ages, but are now only 20 per cent larger, suggesting a growing tendency towards monogamy. But we're not there yet – that 20 per cent difference is compatible with a harem of two to three women, according to biologists.

Women's intuition

Another way for a woman to assess a man is simply to become very skilled at reading all those little signs that signal his real intentions. In fact, brain scans show that when a woman falls in love, various areas of her brain are involved as she makes her evaluation. (By contrast, when a man falls in love, it's the visual area of the brain that's most activated.) So we'd expect women to be better than men at reading emotion in the face and at interpreting body language. And we'd expect men to hone their skills at deceit ('I love you') and be the champions at that.

And, indeed, that seems to be the case. The area of the brain for feeling emotion and reading emotions in others is larger in women than in men. When women chat, they sit closer together than men do and look at one another more directly, while men tend to sit at angles. This skill largely accounts for 'women's intuition' which so mystifies men.

Why men take more risks

See if you can guess the sex of the people involved in the following incidents:

- ▶ The duo who, in 2010 in the little American town of Sedro-Woolley, poured four gallons of methanol into a barrel, sat on top and, in the hope that it would perform something like a rocket, applied a light to the bung hole. (The barrel exploded, killing one of them and seriously injuring the other.)
- ▶ The person who, in an insurance scam, set a car on fire and stabbed their own neck and shoulders to simulate an attack. (Unfortunately, the person cut through an artery and bled to death.)
- ▶ The two bank robbers in Dinant, Belgium, who blew up a cash machine...and themselves with it. (Both died.)

Now there *are* women who take risks. Of course there are. But taking *stupid* risks is almost entirely a male preserve. These people were all nominated for 'Darwin Awards' on a somewhat cynical website that commemorates 'those who improve our gene pool by removing themselves from it'. The more ridiculous, the better. A few women get nominated for the 'award' but by far the majority are men.

Why is this?

Well, as we've already seen, males may have to fight one another for the opportunity to mate with the females. A male too risk-averse to engage in combat would not pass on his genes (unless – and this happens in some species – he can find a more devious route to a coupling). On the other hand, a male willing to take risks would have a greater chance of breeding success. What's more, risky behaviour is a way of demonstrating genetic fitness, and therefore of being chosen by a female.

For the same reason, it's the male of most species that's the most brightly coloured. Bright colours are attractive to the female, but also to predators, so this is another high-risk strategy. In contemporary society, men achieve the same effect by performing dangerous feats (driving fast in sports cars, climbing mountains or building home-made rockets). In evolutionary terms, males can afford it. A woman who dies young will leave few children. A man who dies young can theoretically still father dozens of children if his glamorous risk-taking attracts large numbers of women.

In fact, the most extreme people in just about any field tend to be men. Steven Pinker, the experimental psychologist, defended the President of Harvard University over his remarks on the gender gap in mathematics and science, by pointing out that men are not smarter generally, but are simply more extreme, encompassing both 'more geniuses' as well as 'more idiots'.

Who does the most talking?

Now let me ask you which of the following statements you agree with:

▶ Women speak more than men.
▶ Men speak more than women.
▶ Men and women speak about the same amount.

Given what we know about men competing for sex, and fighting over sex, and given what we know about women being better at reading emotions and being more emotional, we might expect women to use language more extensively. But is that really so?

Careful research has proven that in certain contexts it's actually men who speak more, while in only some contexts do women speak more. Men dominate in what Professor of Linguistics Deborah Tannen calls 'public speaking', also referred to as 'report-talk', while women dominate in 'private speaking' or 'rapport-talk'. That's to say, men speak mostly to convey information and to establish status. In all kinds of public meetings, their voices are heard the most. Women mostly talk to establish connections and create rapport by finding things in common. At home and in social situations, it's their voices that are heard the most.

But when grand totals are compared, there's a very clear winner. Researchers have found that women average 6,000–8,000 words a day, make 2,000–3,000 additional sounds and employ 8,000–10,000 identifiable instances of body language. Men, by contrast, speak only about half as much (2,000–4,000 words), use fewer sounds (1,000–2,000) and employ body language only about a quarter to a third as much (2,000–3,000 gestures). The grand total of daily 'message units' therefore is:

- ▸ women 20,000
- ▸ men 7,000.

Why is it so? On average (and it's important to stress that we are dealing with averages) women have 11 per cent more neurons in their 'language centres' than men do. That's the simple answer. But we still have to know why women's brains evolved that way. Undoubtedly, the survival of women and their children would often have been very reliant on the women's verbal skills. A man out hunting could get by with simple information ('Me go left, you go right'). But if the same man was killed out hunting, his partner would need a greater command of language if she and her children were to survive ('Please think about our suffering. If you help us now, I'll help you if you have problems in the future').

So doesn't social conditioning count for anything?

David Reimer was born as a male identical twin in Winnipeg, Canada in 1965. Both boys were diagnosed with phimosis (non-retraction of the foreskin) and at eight months were circumcised by cauterization. In David's case the operation went wrong and his penis was destroyed. His distraught parents took him to John Money (1921–2006), a psychologist who specialized in gender. Money believed that a child's gender identity was fluid up to a certain age and largely rejected the idea that behavioural differences had a genetic basis. Given that it was much easier to construct a serviceable vagina than a working penis, Money recommended that David should have his testicles removed, be given hormone injections, be brought up as a girl and, when he reached his teenage years, be operated on to create a vagina. David became Brenda.

Money maintained for many years that the gender reassignment was successful, but it wasn't. David/Brenda felt like a boy, wanted to dress and play as other boys did, urinated standing up, and suffered agonies on being forced into a girl's role. He became suicidal and in 1980 his parents were forced to tell him the truth. From then on he began living as a male, had testosterone injections to compensate for the loss of his testicles, and operations to reconstruct a penis. As a young man he married and became stepfather to three children.

But there was to be no happy ending. In 2004 his wife asked for a separation and he committed suicide. Although those feminists who reject the genetic basis for behavioural differences between the sexes can point to David initially being brought up as a boy (before the accident and surgery), this was clearly a misguided experiment that tragically ignored the genetic basis for gender personality differences.

In the next chapter we'll see how exploiting, rather than ignoring, gender personality differences will lead to greater success in love.

10 TIPS FOR SUCCESS

1 Your sex influences many aspects of your personality.

2 Females produce large gametes (sex cells); males produce small ones.

3 Any strategy that increases reproductive success will be selected.

4 Men's and women's most successful breeding strategies are different.

5 Humans are essentially 'machines' built by genes for the benefit of genes.

6 Men breed most successfully when they are easily aroused and promiscuous.

7 Women breed most successfully when they are choosy.

8 Women are co-operative; men are competitive.

9 Men take risks; women talk.

10 Gender differences are much more to do with genes than upbringing.

3

Success in love

In this chapter you will learn:
- *why your face is your fortune*
- *why luck may be better than a wish list*
- *how to keep your relationship going.*

How much can you tell about anyone's personality from their face? It's an important question in life generally, and especially when it comes to dating because it's almost always the face that's the starting point. It takes just one-tenth of a second to decide if we're attracted to someone. After that initial moment, it's very difficult to get us to change our assessments of someone's personality.

Rightly or wrongly, we all make snap judgements about people based on first impressions. What's even more interesting is the similarity of our conclusions, which suggests there must be something in them.

Jokes about dumb blondes notwithstanding, most people assume that attractive men and women will be more capable and intelligent. And it turns out that it's not just prejudice. A team led by the social psychologist Professor Leslie Zebrowitz of Brandeis University in Boston, Massachusetts has demonstrated that there *is* a link between facial attractiveness and intelligence.

Ah yes, you may say, but beauty is in the eye of the beholder. There's no scientific basis to it – fair point. And yet experiments have shown that even babies no more than a few hours old prefer the same faces that adults also consider attractive. So it would appear that beauty *isn't* in the eye of the beholder. It isn't a matter of conditioning. We seem to have an innate sense of what's beautiful.

Insight

Assessing people by their faces is known as physiognomy. Over the centuries, belief in physiognomy has come and gone. Aristotle believed in it, while

Leonardo da Vinci criticized it, and Henry VIII of England tried to stamp it out.

The scientists have applied themselves and come to the conclusion that what we perceive as beauty is nothing more than symmetry. And they have evolutionary logic to prove it. Apparently, people with the most symmetrical faces also tend to have the 'best' genes. Personally, I'm not entirely convinced. Two sticking out ears? Two sets of identical bags under the eyes? And what about the man or woman you first see only in profile but still find attractive? Are the experts missing something?

Be that as it may, researchers have found that women with symmetrical partners have more orgasms than women with asymmetrical partners. Why? Nobody knows for sure. But it seems that symmetrical people, as well as being more attractive, are also more successful. It's part of the female personality, in general, to find such men sexually arousing. But, funnily enough, they don't necessarily want to marry them. At the unconscious level, they seem to feel that symmetrical men are more likely to be unfaithful and less likely to be good fathers. So this all seems to be fitting together.

Another link between appearance and personality was uncovered by a team at the University of Marburg in Germany. They found that among graduates from the famous West Point military academy in the USA, those with the most 'dominant' facial features tended to hold the highest ranks two decades later. Those features, including large jaws and broad cheekbones, are associated with high levels of testosterone at puberty. Testosterone is, of course, the 'male' hormone that, in high quantities, is associated with aggression.

So there seems to be a clear link, via testosterone at puberty, between facial features and dominance. It's not difficult, then, to imagine that mechanisms could be at work much earlier. A team at the Royal College of Surgeons Research Unit in Dublin believes they have proved as much. Using laser scanning techniques, they have found a direct link between the way the brain develops and the way the face develops in the womb. One of the clearest examples comes from those with Down's Syndrome. But those suffering from schizophrenia were also found to be more likely to have certain facial characteristics.

Facing the truth

To see how much weight could be attached to facial features, psychologists at the University of Michigan asked 84 undergraduates who had never met before to rate one another on the Big Five personality traits, based entirely on appearance. For three of the traits, Extroversion, Conscientiousness and Openness, the observers' assessments matched the genuine personality scores more frequently than pure chance. That seemed to suggest that something was going on. But the experiment was criticized by Anthony Little of the University of Stirling, and David Perrett of the University of St Andrews, both in the UK, because it didn't control for non-facial clues such as posture and clothing. They repeated the experiment using photographs and found a link only with Extroversion and Conscientiousness. Not so impressive.

In another experiment, the *New Scientist* magazine invited readers to send in photographs of themselves and complete an online questionnaire. They then made composite images of the people who, according to the questionnaires, were at the extremes of four personality traits – lucky, religious, humorous and trustworthy. The composites were paired up (lucky/unlucky and so on) and readers were invited to examine the pairs online and guess which was which. Over 6,500 readers obliged. The results were surprising.

As regards the women's faces, 73 per cent of readers correctly identified the 'religious' one, and 70 per cent correctly identified the 'lucky' one. But the success rate for trustworthiness was only a little better than chance and the majority of readers were wrong about which composite person was the most humorous.

And when it came to the men's faces, the results were no better than chance. In other words, nothing at all about the *New Scientist*'s four personality traits could be told from men's faces. Possibly men, being generally more impassive than women, don't develop such revealing lines.

It wasn't the most scientific of experiments but it seems to suggest that there's not as much in a face as we think. Even where there does seem to be a connection between face and personality, it's not certain whether the personality causes the face or whether it's our *treatment* of the person with the face that is influential.

In the case of the square-jawed West Point graduates, for example, it may be that these men were simply more aggressive, ambitious and competitive. Or it could be that because they were perceived as more dominant, they were selected for positions of leadership. Similarly, it could be that treating attractive people as intelligent actually causes them to become more intelligent.

Let's leave the last word to the writer George Orwell:

At 50, everyone has the face he deserves.

Insight

Given that judging people by their faces is so universal, there must be some genuine advantage in it. It can be conjectured that earlier in human history an ability to make a quick assessment of a stranger's intentions would have been a survival advantage. But, then again, it's also possible that assessments could become self-fulfilling prophecies. If you assessed a stranger as aggressive and immediately reached for your spear, then the stranger would, indeed, have been likely to behave in a hostile manner. On balance, it might have been better to spear first and ask questions later, rather than to risk exploring what benefits co-operation might bring.

Mirror images

But when it comes to dating, there is something about faces that's vitally important. Even if you're not symmetrical, and even if you're not universally considered attractive, there is a category of men or women who are almost guaranteed to find you strangely alluring. Who are they? They're the ones who look the most like you.

That is, who look as you yourself would look if you were a member of the opposite sex.

I'm not suggesting you have to be the same height or build or literally look like opposite-sex clones. It's more subtle than that. Just study couples who have lived happily together for a few years and you'll see that it's almost always so. There are those same Roman noses, or those same large, sad eyes, or those same voluptuous lips.

If you're not convinced, consider this experiment conducted by Verlin Hinsz, a psychologist at North Dakota State University. Volunteers were asked to look at a collection of photographs and pair up those men and women who, in their opinion, most resembled one another. Many of those men and women were in relationships but the volunteers didn't know which ones. The result was that, far more often than chance, the volunteers paired up the real-life couples.

The clincher comes from Dr Ian Penton-Voak, a psychologist at the University of Stirling, Scotland. He photographed 52 women and, using a computer, masculinized the images. He then showed pictures of various men to each of the women and, unknown to them, included the masculinized versions of their own faces. The result was that the women showed a strong tendency to be attracted to 'themselves'.

> **Insight**
>
> Not only are people attracted to one another on the basis of their similar looks, it seems they also grow to look even more like one another over time. In happy relationships, couples tend to mimic one another's facial expressions, thus developing the same musculature and the same lines.

Various theories have been put forward to account for this. One is that we become accustomed to our own faces and therefore find similar faces familiar and reassuring. Another is that, far from looking for opposites, we actually seek those who most resemble us in every way, including facially. A related possibility is that since we believe faces reflect personalities, we're actually choosing a similar personality when we choose a similar face.

> **Self-coaching tip**
>
> The obvious conclusion to be drawn from all of this is that you'll have more romantic success if you direct your attention to people who look like you.

Why most lists don't work

One enchanted evening, in the words of the song, you look across a crowded room and...wham! You're in love. You probably don't need me to tell you the physical signs of attraction and infatuation but here they are anyway:

- exhilaration
- sleeplessness
- loss of appetite
- butterflies in the stomach
- stammering and awkwardness
- dilated pupils
- pounding heart
- dizziness
- weak knees.

But not so fast. Yes, it could well be that you've encountered your opposite sex face. And that's a good start. But other things could be going on as well.

That instant feeling of attraction has no intellectual component. Not yet, anyway. For the moment, it's all in the limbic system, the most 'primitive' part of the brain. The higher brain isn't involved. In fact, it's almost as if it's disconnected. Not the sort of condition in which to take an important decision.

Maybe you should make a list of all the things you need in a partner before you set off. That way you can avoid embarking on a relationship you think is so right but which all your cool-headed friends can see is so wrong. In the internet age, it's certainly a common tactic.

If you were to make one, what would be on yours? Ugly face? Awful sense of humour? Overweight? Cruel? Unemployed with huge debts? Hardly. And that's one of the problems with lists. We all tend to write down the same kinds of things to do with beauty, kindness, money and so on which are actually fairly meaningless – and unattainable. We fall back on stereotypes. Physical things are more important to most men than to most women, so a typical man's list would include firm, medium-sized breasts, hourglass figure, good teeth, and probably a particular hair colour. Women are more interested in personality, wealth and status, so a typical woman's list would include a good sense of humour, a well-paid job, and the respect of other people.

But not everyone can marry an attractive, kind person with a great sense of humour, an apartment in Mayfair, an estate in Cornwall and a yacht in the Caribbean. And those that do are not necessarily very happy, as relationship therapists and divorce lawyers can testify.

But, anyway, let's suppose you've drawn up your list and, perhaps at a speed-dating night, met two potential partners. After totting up their scores, you see that Candidate A meets 99 of your 100 listed requirements while Candidate B meets 90. So it's fairly obvious that Candidate A wins. Right? But supposing Candidate B's failings were all fairly trivial, while Candidate A's single failing was something fundamental to your happiness. Suppose you desperately want children but Candidate A wants nothing to do with them? Suppose you want to live near your family but Candidate A wants to emigrate. Suppose you have a strong sex drive but Candidate A has a weak one? These are all things that could wreck a relationship, no matter how many other things you agree on.

So you need a system of weighting...

It's all getting rather complicated, isn't it? Better to throw that sort of list away. Here, instead, is a list that works, based on all that we know about successful relationships:

▶ The same educational, social and family background
▶ The same beliefs about politics, religion, freedom and social justice
▶ The same goals
▶ The same vision of the life you want to lead
▶ The same vision of how things should be in five, ten, twenty and fifty years
▶ The same interests and passions
▶ The same feelings about sex.

And:
▶ The same but opposite-sex face.

> ### Self-coaching tip
>
> Opposites may attract but, in human life, they don't stay together.

Finding 'the One'

So you're almost ready to set off. You're looking for someone with a face like yours, with a background like yours, a present like yours, and a vision of the future like yours. You're on a mission to find 'The One'. But there's something very important you must know.

'The One' does not exist.

Even the most romantic of us only describe our partners as one in a million. Applying that ratio to the population of the planet still provides you with a choice of several hundred. But, in reality, you certainly don't need to date a million people to find someone you can be very, very happy with. You don't even need to date a thousand. Nor in all probability a hundred.

For the mathematically minded among you, statisticians have worked out that the perfect strategy is to date a dozen people and then to select the very next person who is better than any of the 12. You should have found your mate before 40 dates.

I'm not suggesting you actually do that. I'm just throwing it in to illustrate the point that there are a lot of people with whom you could be happy, not just 'One'. In real life the 12-plus strategy only sort-of works. Because you still have to know what 'better' means.

We probably all know someone who has broken up with a spouse, a boyfriend, or girlfriend and fairly soon begun dating a person with the same looks and personality. You've probably done it yourself. Again, and again...and again. The fact is, we all seem to have inside us somewhere the template for this 'ideal partner'. Except that it isn't. Not from the point of view of happiness or stability, anyway.

Quite possibly the template is nature's way of matchmaking the best genetic fit. Quite possibly it is all to do with 'unfinished business'. But neither of those things is a sound basis for a loving and happy relationship.

So what is?

The fact is that most of us don't have a very accurate idea of the kind of person we could love and live with for the rest of our lives. Not until, that is, that person comes along and we do fall in love and live happily ever after. Then we can say, so *that's* the kind of person for me.

Asking a young person to identify the essential characteristics of 'the One' is a little like asking what features you would like to have included on a new planet. Until you've experienced every kind of possibility you just can't say.

So my advice is this. Let chance enter your dating life. Go out with someone you're *not* attracted to. You may well discover that the person who seemed all wrong is utterly, utterly right.

Society has, apparently, changed quite a lot in a few years. In 1939, American men said love was only their fourth priority when it came to a relationship, while for American women it was fifth. (If you want to know what came first, men's priority was a dependable character, while women were looking for emotional maturity.) Now, both men and women say love is the number one priority. Assuming those were both accurate surveys, they point to a fascinating change in quite a short time.

THE SWEET SMELL OF SUCCESS

So let's get back to that crowded room. You've seen someone you feel drawn to. You stroll over. You say 'hello'. ('Hello', research shows, is as good a way of kicking off as anything, so there's no need to bother with chat-up lines.) And then...nothing. No electricity. What's wrong?

The answer could be the way you smell.

It has nothing to do with failings in your personality, nor anything to do with personal hygiene, but something more cunning. It turns out that your smell is an advert for your body's genetically programmed defences; specifically, the fifty or so genes known as the major histo compatibility complex (MHC). This takes us back to evolution, Darwin, and all the rest of it. Neither of you may be the least bit interested in having children, but even so you can't escape the way natural selection has put things together.

MHC is what is known as codominant, which means children inherit active versions of the genes from both parents. If you and your partner have different MHC, then your children will have immunity to a greater range of diseases.

A man isn't too concerned about this but, unconsciously, a woman is. She's programmed to mate with a man whose MHC is very different to hers, because her children will then have the best chance of surviving and flourishing. And, amazingly, she doesn't need to send a sample of his DNA to a laboratory. All she has to do is smell him.

We know this because a Swiss scientist called Claus Wedekind asked women to apply their noses to men's T-shirts. The more the woman's own MHC differed from the man's, the more she found his smell pleasant and sexy. But there were two exceptions. The first was that the man's MHC shouldn't be *too* different. The second was for women taking the Pill.

It turned out that women on hormonal contraceptives actually preferred men with *similar* MHC. In fact, that's logical because those contraceptives make a woman's body act as if she's pregnant. She's now no longer interested in mating. Instead she's looking for the safety of men who smell like she does. Say, her father.

So the Pill may be playing havoc with mate selection. The man a woman finds attractive when she's on the Pill is the man she finds unattractive when she's off the Pill. And again there's scientific evidence to back this up. Studies show that the closer a couple's MHC profiles, the more the woman is likely to be unfaithful.

Getting a date

How difficult is it for a woman to seduce a man? Not very. In one experiment, an attractive woman approached men on an American college campus and asked if they would like to have sex. Three-quarters of the men accepted.

How difficult is it for a man to seduce a woman? Fairly difficult. When the experiment was done the other way around and an attractive man approached women and asked if they would like to have sex, not a single woman accepted. Not one.

That's the part of the story that gets the headlines. And given what we learned in the last chapter about the difference between male and female mating strategies, we shouldn't be surprised. But there is a more interesting and surprising part. If simply asked for a date, half of men and women agreed. In other words, for every two people you ask out on a date, one will accept, always provided, that is, that you fit the description of 'attractive'.

So the personality traits of the most successful daters are looking like this:

▶ High in Extroversion (to dare to ask)
▶ High in Agreeableness (to skilfully progress beyond the original request)
▶ Low in Neuroticism (so you're not demoralized by the inevitable rejections).

That's not to say you can't be entirely successful if you're the opposite of those things, but you're going to have to struggle with yourself a lot more.

MONEY MAKES UP FOR A LOT

And supposing you don't merit that 'attractive' tag? Well, there are quite a few things you can do, in psychological terms, to make yourself more desirable. But before we come to those, there's a rather difficult subject I can't avoid, although I'd like to. It's not for nothing that the dating scene is often described as a marketplace. And that, indeed, is how it tends to operate. In effect, we all have a value. And, as we'll see in a moment, we can actually put a price on it – in pounds or dollars or whatever currency you like.

What it means is that you should be proposing dates to people who have more or less the same value as yourself. Let's say that on a scale of 1 to 100 you have a value of 30. Then you're very unlikely to have that one in two success rate if you ask out people who have a score of, say, 80. But stick to people around your own level of 30 and you very likely will succeed half the time.

It all seems very cold and even horrible. But I'm only the messenger. I'm not saying this is how people should behave, only that it's how people tend to behave. Economists have worked out that in America:

▶ women require a man to earn an extra $30,000 a year for each inch that he's below six feet tall

▶ to enjoy the same success with white women that a white man enjoys, a Hispanic man has to earn an extra $77,000 a year, an African-American $154,000 a year, and an Asian man $247,000 a year

▶ a man considered to be in the bottom 10 per cent in terms of physical attractiveness needs to earn $186,000 a year extra to put him in the top 10 per cent overall

▶ there's no amount of money that can raise a physically unattractive woman into the top 10 per cent.

Self-coaching tip

It's a very bad strategy for a man to let it be known that he's primarily looking for sex. A man has to show (or pretend) he's interested in the woman as a person. A woman's strategy is more complicated. A date is guaranteed if sex is guaranteed. But by making herself seem 'easy' she rules herself out as a serious partner. Her best strategy, then, is flirtation – tantalizing a man with the prospect of sex but not actually allowing it until he's demonstrated his seriousness.

Money aside, what can you do to make yourself more attractive in non-physical terms? Actually, it isn't difficult. All you have to do (without in any way seeming desperate) is make it plain that you find the other person very attractive, that you admire them, that you find them witty, amusing and intelligent, and that you share their interests, goals and concerns. In other words, if you're not high in Agreeableness, learn to fake it (or see Chapter 13 for how to make a genuine improvement).

The following psychological tricks will help.

Priming

It turns out that our opinion of other people has a lot to do with the setting in which we see them. This won't come as any great surprise. But you may be taken aback by the *extent* to which this is true. In one experiment, people tended to be viewed as cold merely if they handed out cold drinks, while they were seen as warm if they handed out hot drinks. So give very careful thought to the places you meet and the accessories you bring, because they're going to reflect on the way your personality is perceived.

Do something (slightly) dangerous

It appears that fear/pain and sexual arousal are closely linked. That's why some people enjoy sadomasochistic games and there's undoubtedly a connection with the way some male animals bite the neck of the females when mating. In one experiment, men in Vancouver were met by a woman interviewer who asked some innocuous questions about the environment and then gave her telephone number on the pretext that the men might want to talk further about the study. Those men who had just crossed the high, wobbly Capilano Canyon Suspension Bridge were eight times more likely to phone than men who had crossed by a safer bridge. However, don't do anything so dangerous that your date can't enjoy the occasion. A frisson is enough.

Create an intense moment

According to Nobel prizewinning psychologist Daniel Kahneman, your date will have strong memories of just two incidents. One would be a moment of intense emotion. So make sure the emotion is happiness. If something should go badly wrong on the date, the best way of overriding that memory is to counter it with something even more intensely positive.

End on a high

According to Mr Kahneman, the other memory your date will recall is the way the date ended. Anyone who ever produced a musical knows how important that final chorus is. So don't let the date peter out with a trudge back to one home or the other and a miserably nervous kiss on the doorstep. Orchestrate a climax – and immediately go your separate ways.

> **Insight**
> In one survey, dating couples were found to have lied to one another in about one-third of the things they said. Keep that in mind. Men are a little more likely to lie than women, and women are a little more likely to spot lies than men.

Keeping that relationship going

Fast-forward a few years. One date led to another. You got together and time passed. What happens now? Do you live happily ever after? Or unhappily ever after? Or do you split and try again? In America, the likelihood that newlyweds will remain together until one of them dies stands at about 30 per cent. In other words, seven out of ten people getting married in America this week will break up. And figures are similar throughout much of the Western world. What are your own chances? If you want to know what the future holds for your relationship, read on.

BEING MONOGAMOUS HELPS

It's sometimes said that an affair is good for a married relationship. Well, yes, some men would say that, wouldn't they! But funnily enough, there hasn't yet been a case of anyone asking for a divorce on the grounds that their partner *hasn't* had an affair. On the other hand, there are plenty of the opposite.

For some people, the barriers to infidelity are high. For others they're low. Here are some of the ways you can tell in advance.

▶ Partners high in Openness are very much more likely to be unfaithful than partners low in Openness.
▶ Partners low on Conscientiousness are more likely to be unfaithful than partners high in Conscientiousness.

- ▶ Partners high in Extroversion are more likely to be unfaithful than partners low in Extroversion.
- ▶ Partners low on Agreeableness are more likely to be unfaithful than partners high in Agreeableness .
- ▶ Partners whose parents were unfaithful are more likely to be unfaithful.

Insight

When one or both parents are unfaithful, their children are less likely to be monogamous, partly for cultural reasons but also very much for genetic reasons. Anyone who has inherited the novelty-seeking form of the serotonin transporter gene, for example, is more likely to be unfaithful. The same goes for any man whose genes have coded for a reduced number of vasopressin receptors in the brain, or for women who are deficient in oxytocin. There's much more about the effect of genes in Chapter 10.

Self-coaching tip

Never tell a man that you'd be willing to overlook an affair – you're almost guaranteeing that he'll have one. Or two. Or three.

TRIANGULAR LOVE

The psychologist Robert Sternberg has proposed that love can be modelled as a triangle (he's also proposed the same for intelligence). He believes it has three components – intimacy, passion and commitment.

- ▶ **Consummate** love can only develop over time. You feel all three components strongly and in equal proportions – in other words, you have large, matching equilateral triangles. Such couples delight in one another's company. As to passion, Sternberg considers the test is that you're still having great sex after fifteen years. (If you'd still like to be having great sex after 25 or 50 years, you might like to read *Have Great Sex*, also in the Teach Yourself series.)
- ▶ **Non-love** is at the opposite end of the scale to consummate love. That is, you feel none of the three components.
- ▶ **Liking** means you feel a degree of intimacy but neither passion nor commitment. In other words, this is how you feel about close friends.

▶ **Infatuation** comes about in the early stages of a romance. You feel overwhelmed by passion but both intimacy and commitment are weak.

▶ **Empty** love is Sternberg's phrase for the sort of relationship where commitment is high but both passion and intimacy are low. It's the situation of some long-term married people who are determined to stay together for the sake of the children or to preserve certain aspects of their lifestyle but who feel no passion and are not intimate.

▶ **Romantic** love is the love of those who have been together only a short while. They're intimate and they feel passion but they haven't experienced enough together to feel a strong sense of commitment.

▶ **Companionate** love is the situation of many older married couples. They understand one another very well, they enjoy being together and they intend to stay together, but sexual passion has waned.

▶ **Fatuous** love is Sternberg's description of the kind of situation in which two people, driven by passion, get married after a short romance. The sex is electric and a commitment has been made but the two can't know one another very well. Intimacy can develop over time but, on the other hand, as the lovers get to know one another better, they may not like what they find.

Here's a little test that I've compiled. Rate how you stand on each criterion on a scale of 1 to 10, where 1 means 'not at all' and 10 means 'enormously':

  1 I feel very close to my partner.
  2 Everything I have I share with my partner.
  3 I communicate very well with my partner.
  4 My partner understands me.
  5 I don't feel the need to hide anything from my partner.
  6 I would rather be with my partner than with anyone else.
  7 I think about my partner frequently during the day.
  8 When I hear romantic music I think about my partner.
  9 I fantasize about my partner.
 10 I love having sex with my partner.
 11 I feel that my decision to live with my partner was the best decision I ever made.
 12 I expect my love for my partner to last all my life.

13 I feel a sense of responsibility for my partner.

14 Even if another person was strongly attracted to me, I know I would never be unfaithful to my partner.

15 I am certain that I love my partner.

How you scored

Your total score gives you the strength of your love, ranging from 15 to 150. But we can go a little further. The first five questions were all about intimacy, the next five all about passion, and the final five all about commitment. Assuming you and your partner both scored somewhat less than 150, it's important to know how the points were distributed between the three components of love. You could both have total scores of 100, for example, but if one of you scored 40 for passion and the other 10, then you're not very compatible. Remember, your triangle and your partner's triangle should ideally be the same shapes.

So separate out the scores by the first, second and third groups of five questions and see how the shapes of your triangles compare.

HOW YOU SCORED ON INTIMACY

5–20: You keep lots of things hidden, partly to retain some sense of independence and partly because there are things you would be embarrassed for your partner to know. You live together but there's a considerable distance between you. If you're to avoid drifting apart, you need to open up more.

21–35: You have the same degree of intimacy with your partner that's normal for most couples, but there are still things that you hide. You don't feel you can be completely yourself and that's a stress. There's no need to rush at it but, over time, try to discuss your deepest feelings more openly with your partner.

36–50: You're very high on intimacy and gain a great deal of emotional support as a result.

HOW YOU SCORED ON PASSION

5–20: The passion has definitely gone out of your relationship. Unless there's some medical reason why one or both of you can't have sex, and have it often, then this is something you should discuss. Are you both happy with the situation? If not, you need to explore the ways passion can be reignited.

21–35: Your feelings of passion are in the mainstream. Probably you've been together a little while and some of the excitement has gone. But it doesn't have to be that way. First of all, examine your relationship to see if there are any resentments that are holding you back. If not, get yourselves a good sex manual (see *Have Great Sex* or *Get Intimate with Tantric Sex* from the Teach Yourself series) and introduce some new ideas.

36–50: You obviously feel a great deal of passion. Possibly you and your partner haven't been together very long. But if you've been together more than 15 years, then your continuing passion shows that it can be done.

HOW YOU SCORED ON COMMITMENT

5–20: You may be deriving a great deal of pleasure from your relationship but at the moment you obviously don't feel your partner is someone very special to you.

21–35: You feel committed to your partner but only while things are going well. If there were to be problems in the relationship, you might look elsewhere rather than try to overcome them.

36–50: You obviously have a very solid relationship. You intend to stick with it even through bad times, whatever they might be. Hopefully it's also high on intimacy and passion, in which case you're extremely lucky.

Your sexual personality

There's an old saying that problems in a relationship start in bed. So let's see how compatible you are sexually. Both of you should privately select the answers that most closely resemble your own views, then compare. Be honest, otherwise there's no point in completing the questionnaire.

1 Solo masturbation is:
   a quite different to sex with another person and something I enjoy.
   b a rather sad perversion.
2 Fantasizing about sex is:
   a something I enjoy.
   b a sign that something is wrong in a relationship.

3 Oral sex is:
    a a great technique for increasing excitement.
    b unhygienic.
4 Sleeping naked is:
    a sensual and intimate.
    b inappropriate and usually cold.
5 Sex purely for enjoyment is:
    a a great thing.
    b immoral.
6 For a great sex life:
    a you need to keep trying new techniques.
    b you should stick to the things you know you enjoy.
7 Sex can be:
    a a very spiritual experience.
    b nothing more than a physical experience.
8 I would like to have sex:
    a most days.
    b only when it feels like a special occasion.
9 Genitals are:
    a beautiful – I like to look and am happy to be looked at.
    b ugly and best kept under the bedclothes.
10 Sex is:
    a very important to me.
    b something I can take or leave.

It won't have escaped your notice that all the a's reveal enthusiasm for sex and a fairly liberal attitude, whereas all the b's indicate less enthusiasm and more conservative attitude. If you both scored roughly the same proportion of 'a's and 'b's, then you're fairly compatible in bed.

Insight

In a study in San Francisco, before the AIDS epidemic, three-quarters of gay men said they had had over one hundred lovers and 28 per cent said they had had sex with over one thousand. By contrast, only 2 per cent of lesbians reported more than a hundred lovers. Some have interpreted the figures as showing that men and women have different sexual appetites and that heterosexual men would have far more busy and varied sex lives if women were of the same mind. Or it could just be that, for whatever reason, homosexual men have a different attitude than heterosexual men.

Here's another test:

- ▶ Over the next month (or for the past month, if you can remember) record the number of times you have sex.
- ▶ Over the next month (or for the past month, if you can remember) record the number of times you have an argument.

The greater the frequency of sex relative to the frequency of arguments, the happier your relationship and the more likely it is to endure.

Emotional intelligence

There's not much point in staying together if you don't share the same interests, the same outlook, the same goals, and so on. But suppose your relationship is in trouble despite the fact that you *do*? Then surely it's worth saving.

As we've already seen, lots of men and women begin new relationships with someone very similar to the person they've just rejected. That could be a shame. A lot of heartache for nothing. It could be better to try what psychologist Daniel Goleman has dubbed 'emotional intelligence' rather than a new partner.

What is it that makes a new relationship work where the old one didn't, if only for a time? Quite simply, people make more effort to be amenable when a relationship is new. That's to say, they make more effort to control their moods, to rein in negative impulses, to be empathetic, to be conciliatory rather than confrontational, and to snuff out arguments before they go too far. It's this that is emotional intelligence and some of us have more than others (and women in general have more than men). If you're high in the Big Five trait of Agreeableness, then you'll naturally have a high emotional intelligence, too. But it's also something that can be cultivated.

John Gottman, professor emeritus of psychology at the University of Washington, is very good at spotting the signs of emotional intelligence, as well as a few other things. In fact, he's become so good at reading the signs that when couples come to his 'Love Lab' he can predict divorce within the next three years with 94 per cent accuracy.

You may not have Gottman's experience. On the other hand, you have access to information he can only guess at. These are the key indicators for impending separation:

▶ One of you makes a personal criticism.
▶ One of you becomes defensive.
▶ One of you becomes contemptuous.
▶ One of you becomes withdrawn.

If all four are occurring regularly, your relationship is in serious trouble. Experts call them 'The Four Horsemen of the Apocalypse'. Why? You guessed it. Because they herald the end.

BEATING THE HORSEMEN

It's seldom too late to beat those horsemen away if that's what *you both really want*. Let's start with how to handle differences regarding behaviour.

Relationship experts say you should never make *personal* attacks on your partner, but that criticizing your partner's *behaviour* is allowed. I'd go further. So here's the first rule:
▶ Don't criticize *at all*.

Criticism implies disapproval. It implies moral superiority. No one likes to be on the receiving end, whether the criticism is couched in a personal way ('You're a pig for leaving your clothes on the floor') or more obliquely ('Leaving clothes on the floor is piggish behaviour'). It all amounts to the same thing.

Let's say your partner does, indeed, leave clothes on the floor. Well, your partner is an adult. Your partner equally shares the home with you. Your partner is as entitled to leave clothes on the floor as you're entitled to hang yours in a cupboard. Which brings me to the next point:
▶ Acceptance.

Acceptance is the secret of successful relationships. According to research, two-thirds of couples never resolve their disagreements. So agreeing to disagree is an essential part of remaining together.

But what happens when there are things you just can't accept? You've got to do something, especially as two more very important rules are:

- Communicate
- Don't harbour resentments – discuss your feelings.

So you've got to take some sort of action. But that still doesn't mean you're entitled to *criticize*. You could simply hang your partner's clothes up yourself. Is that such a terrible thing to do? (Hopefully, your partner is also doing things for you.) Or you could explain that you find untidiness upsetting. Or that clothes on the floor collect dust which brings on your asthma attacks. Do you see the difference? You're discussing your feelings but you're not criticizing.

If emotions take over and a discussion starts to get out of hand, diffuse the situation with a joke, or agree to return to the subject after a coffee-break.

Here's the next point:
- Discover your partner's finest qualities.

Researchers have discovered that in happy long-term relationships the partners have higher opinions of each other than outsiders think are warranted. It's summed up in that well-known phrase: 'I can't see what he/she sees in her/him.' It's sometimes known as 'wearing rose-tinted glasses'. But it isn't that at all. Contented partners simply have a different way of looking at things, a way that's less cynical, less judgemental and more profound. Being loved by someone else is a terrific thing and not to be treated lightly.

Finally, research shows that boredom is a major factor in the break-up of any relationship. Partners high in Extroversion particularly seek novelty. So:
- Avoid boredom.

Keep trying new things together, and doing exciting things together, out of the bedroom and in.

> **Insight**
> If you can articulate what it is about your partner that attracts you, if you can articulate why you love your partner, then that probably isn't the real reason at all. The fact is, these are the kinds of things that just can't be articulated.

10 TIPS FOR SUCCESS

1 The face isn't a very good guide to personality.

2 We're all attracted to opposite-sex versions of our own faces.

3 Instant attraction is in the limbic system, the brain's most 'animal' part.

4 Making lists of desirable personality traits and other qualities is usually a waste of time.

5 'The One' does not exist.

6 Simply by asking for a date, and assuming that you're reasonably attractive, you'll be successful about half the time.

7 You'll be more successful if you date people with the same 'market value' as yourself.

8 The risk of infidelity is, in part, genetically determined.

9 The higher the frequency of lovemaking compared with the frequency of arguments the better the relationship.

10 Don't criticize one another.

4

....

Personality poppycock?

In this chapter you will learn:
* *which popular personality beliefs are true*
* *why you may get an undeserved blot on your character*
* *how so much is explained by the Forer Effect.*

In the late eighteenth century, German physician Franz Joseph Gall developed a new discipline he called phrenology. Gall believed that character, thoughts and emotions are contained in the brain, that specific parts of the brain have specific functions, and that the degree to which those functions are developed is reflected in the shape of the skull above those brain regions.

Gall would run his fingers over patients' skulls, feeling for bumps and indentations. From these he would assess which of the 27 'organs' of the brain were well-developed and which were under-developed.

Half a century later, phrenology was given a boost by a bizarre accident.

The strange case of Phineas Gage
On 13 September 1848, Phineas Gage was blasting rock for the construction of the Rutland and Burlington Railroad in Vermont. As foreman it was his job to place the blasting powder and tamp it down with an iron rod. He had done it hundreds of times before but, on this occasion, for some reason, the powder exploded, launching the iron tamping rod right through his head. It entered just below his left eye and exited through the top of his skull, landing 80 feet away, and taking part of Gage's left frontal lobe with it.

Amazingly, Gage survived and went on to live for almost 12 more years. What was equally amazing was that he was still able to function, subsequently working in livery stables and as a stagecoach driver. But, of course, he wasn't quite the same old Gage that he had been.

Along with part of his left frontal lobe, Gage had lost the ability to control his impulses. From being a man high in Conscientiousness he had become a man low in Conscientiousness, stubborn, foul-mouthed and unreliable. According to Dr John Martyn Harlow who treated him, Gage's 'animal propensities' had free rein.

A century later, an equally colourful case again illustrated how brain damage could impact 'animal propensities'.

In 1943, Margaret Sweeney fell 40 feet down a lift shaft in Bond Street, tearing her fingernails out as she clutched at the lift cable, damaging her knees and cracking her head. As a result she lost her sense of taste and smell and, it seems, her inhibitions. In 1963, she was sued for divorce by her second husband, the 11th Duke of Argyll. The case caused a sensation. He cited 88 lovers, including two cabinet ministers and three members of the royal family, and, as part of his evidence, produced the Polaroid photographs the press tantalizingly dubbed the 'headless man'.

The man was headless only in the sense that the camera had been aimed low. One photograph showed the Duchess crouching, naked except for her signature necklace of three strands of pearls, performing fellatio. The other showed a man masturbating. The case was too involved to explore the full details here, but there were rumours the photographs showed not one man but two, Douglas Fairbanks Jr, the actor, and Duncan Sandys, the then Minister of Defence and son-in-law of Winston Churchill. Certainly Polaroid cameras were then very rare and there was said to be only one in Britain at the time – on loan to the Ministry of Defence.

Where is personality?

Nowadays, using brain-imaging techniques, we know for a fact that the frontal lobes are very involved with personality. They're certainly connected with social and sexual behaviour, the control of impulses and judgement, so Gage's 'animal propensities' and the Duchess's promiscuity were exactly what might be expected.

We also know, for example, that people high in Conscientiousness have larger lateral prefrontal cortices, and that those high in Extroversion have larger medial orbitofrontal cortices. We know that the amygdala (a pea-sized area in the centre of the brain) reacts when anyone sees a threatening face, but that only the amygdalas of those high in Extroversion light up for happy faces. And we know that brain development has some impact on the shape of the skull as well as the face.

So was Dr Gall correct? Well, for his era his insights were remarkable. But phrenology, as described by him, is no more useful than astrology. That's to say, not at all (see below).

The Rorschach ink-blot test

To overcome the failings of conventional self-reporting personality tests (see Chapter 1), many psychologists use what are known as 'projective' techniques. These kinds of tests work on the basis that personality is primarily unconscious.

The most famous of them is the Rorschach ink-blot test. Invented by the Swiss psychologist Hermann Rorschach in the 1920s, it consists of a series of ten standardized blots with almost perfect bilateral symmetry – five are black, two are black and red and three are multicoloured. The psychologist takes note of what you see in the images as well as other factors, such as how long it takes you to respond, whether or not you rotate the cards, whether or not you ask if you can rotate the cards, and anything you say.

The Thematic Apperception Test (TAT) is another projective test, developed a decade after the Rorschach. In place of inkblots, TAT uses a series of pictures (31 in all, but most psychologists select around ten). The subject is asked to create as dramatic a story as possible around each picture including:

▶ what happened before the picture
▶ what's going on in the picture
▶ what people in the picture are thinking and feeling
▶ what happened after the picture.

So are these projective tests more accurate than the self-reporting variety? The answer seems to be 'no'. The psychologists Scott Lilienfeld, James Wood and Howard Garb investigated the Rorschach and published their findings in the journal *Psychological*

Science in the Public Interest in 2000. They concluded that the test was too subjective, since psychologists frequently disagreed over interpretation. What's more, in their study, the Rorschach failed to accurately identify a wide range of mental problems including anxiety disorders, depression, and psychopathic personality. Nor did it correctly pick out children who had been sexually abused – a task for which it was believed to be especially suited.

You and your stars

In both Britain and America a majority think 'there's something in' astrology. There isn't.

Astrologers point out that oysters open and close in accordance with the tides, which are determined by the electromagnetic and gravitational forces of the sun and moon. Quite so. What they fail to point out is that the effect is uniform, affecting *all* oysters in the same area equally, irrespective of when they were 'born'.

In any event, how is the all-important moment of birth to be judged? Is it when the head first appears, or when the baby is entirely free of the vagina, or when the cord is cut, or what? Why should the moment of birth be critical, but not the moment of conception? And if the baby is due on the 4th May but, for whatever reason, is born on the 4th April, does that mean its personality is somehow changed? By what mechanism?

Some astrologers argue that planetary phenomena don't necessarily cause events but are merely synchronous with them. Identifying the phenomena, therefore, makes it possible to anticipate the other synchronous events. The proposed mechanism for this is that there's a much larger 'framework' behind everything, a position championed by the Swiss psychologist Carl Jung (1875–1961). An analogy would be that the light goes off in your lounge and you then discover that it's also gone off in the hall. The light going off in the lounge didn't *cause* the light to go off in the hall. The events are synchronous and due to something happening in the 'framework' which, in this case, is the electricity supply.

In his book *Synchronicity*, Jung described how while a client was describing a dream involving a golden scarab, a beetle identified as a rose chafer (*Cetonia aurata*) flew into his window. Although he stated that 'nothing like it ever happened to me before or since', Jung chose to take it as a clear example of synchronicity. Critics, of whom I am one, see it instead as a clear example of confirmation bias. Jung, who grew up in a household where the supernatural was believed in, saw what he wanted to see. For more on confirmation bias, take a look at Chapter 6.

> **Insight**
>
> In fact, the equinox and solstice points have moved about 30 degrees westwards in the past 2,000 years which means that had you been born on the same day and at the same time two millennia ago you would have had a different birth sign to today's.

But if there's nothing in astrology, why do so many people find that the analyses and predictions turn out to be correct. The answer to that is the Forer Effect. Bertram Forer (1914–2000) was a psychologist who took a personality analysis from an astrology column and presented it to people without regard to their star signs. Nevertheless, the average rating across all subjects was that the analysis was highly accurate. The astrologer (or magician or mentalist) says things that are made to sound specific but which are, in fact, universal. An example would be that 'you like other people to admire you but are often critical of yourself' or that you have 'considerable untapped potential' or that you're 'sometimes extroverted but at other times introverted'.

Not convinced? Just look at the hard evidence. Astrologers do not, themselves, make fortunes on the stock market or at the roulette wheel or by betting on horses. In one experiment, 30 leading astrologers were given the birth details of one person and provided with three personality profiles to choose from. They were less successful than chance.

> **Insight**
>
> Scientific studies have found one personality effect related to *season* of birth. Babies born in the autumn and winter in northern Europe score higher on novelty-seeking (high Extraversion) than those born in the spring and summer.

Self-coaching tip

Don't take notice of astrology. But do take notice of the way other people are influenced by the Forer Effect.

Birth order

Out of the first 23 astronauts into space, 21 were first-borns. This is just one example of the anecdotal evidence that convinces many people that birth order matters. And it seems logical. First-borns are usually 'spoiled'. A child with an older sibling has to learn to fight and to carve out a distinctive personality. The last-born is 'babied', and so on.

But even the anecdotal evidence is pretty thin, causing child expert Judith Rich Harris to limit birth order effects to within the family circle, but not outside it. In other words, the last-born may play the baby of the family at family gatherings, even in middle age, but behave differently in other contexts.

The problem is that very little reliable scientific research has been done either to back up the birth order hypothesis or to disprove it. The best evidence we have is that in 2007, Norwegians Petter Kristensen and Tor Bjerkedal published work showing a *small* correlation between birth order and IQ – the lower your birth-order ranking, the lower your IQ is likely to be. And in 2009, Joshua Hartshorne, then a student at Harvard, published data suggesting that birth order influences whom we choose as friends and spouses. First-borns tend to pair up with first-borns, middles with middles, only children with only children, and so on.

And that's about it.

The problem for research in this field is that there are always a mass of other factors that are difficult to disentangle. For example, large families tend to be lower on the socio-economic ladder. So third-borns will, on average, come from poorer families than first-borns.

The consensus is that any effects seem to be small and not enduring into adult life, with one notable exception – sexual orientation.

BIRTH ORDER AND SEXUAL ORIENTATION

The pioneering sex researcher Alfred Kinsey (1894–1956) concluded that sexual orientation could be viewed as a continuum and introduced a scale on which 0 represents those who are exclusively heterosexual and 6 those who are exclusively homosexual. Some people are at one end and some at the other, but quite a lot of people lie along the continuum somewhere between the two.

Statistics suggest that there is a one-third increase in the likelihood of a man being at the homosexual end of the continuum for every older brother. This is not so much to do with upbringing as to the curious fact that women increasingly produce anti-male antibodies with each successive pregnancy. However, the effect does not seem to apply to left-handed homosexual men. Intriguingly, homosexual men have a one-third higher chance of being left-handed than heterosexual men, while lesbians have almost double the chance compared with heterosexual women.

But birth order is just one possible effect:

▶ The geneticist Dean Hamer has identified a chromosomal marker, a so-called 'gay gene' that may cause some men to be homosexual or, at least, to lean towards homosexuality as a choice.

▶ Another theory is that it has to do with androgens (male hormones) in the womb. If an egg is fertilized by a sperm carrying a Y chromosome, the foetus will twice be flooded with androgens, at an interval of about a month, causing the development of male sexual organs and a masculinized brain. If that process doesn't proceed in the standard way (some foetuses, for example, exhibit Androgen Insensitivity Syndrome), then it's possible to have a male brain trapped in a woman's body or a female brain trapped in a man's body.

But there's no reason, anyway, to assume that there is one identical cause in every case. One thing for sure is that it's hard, if not impossible, to change a homosexual man's sexual orientation through psychological techniques. It's been tried many times and just about always fails. However, it seems that for women, lesbianism may be more of a choice.

Finger it out

If you want to know how much exposure you had to androgens (male hormones such as testosterone) in the womb, you can 'finger it out' by comparing the relative lengths of your second and fourth fingers. The difference is more marked on the right hand, so that's the hand that is used. In men, the second digit (forefinger/index finger) tends to be shorter than the fourth digit (the ring finger), while in women the second digit is the same size as, or slightly longer than, the fourth.

Here's what you do:

1 Turn your right hand palm side up and measure the second finger (forefinger/index finger) from the base to the tip.
2 Measure the fourth finger (ring finger) in the same way.
3 Divide the length of the second finger (forefinger/index finger) by the length of the fourth finger (ring finger), e.g. second finger 8cm ÷ fourth finger 9cm = 0.889. Men usually have a ratio of less than one, while women usually have a ratio of one or more.

Some scientists believe the ratio is a marker for masculine and feminine traits. So a low ratio (relatively longer fourth finger) would be associated with competitiveness, aggression, sporting prowess and so on.

Studies show that lesbians tend to have masculine ratios, while homosexual men have either hyper-masculinized or feminized ratios, supporting the view that sexual preference may be related to the degree of androgen exposure in the womb.

Self-coaching tip

The really important point in all this is that your sexual preference seems to be an innate part of who you are. You should never deny it or be ashamed of it.

You and your handwriting

Everything you do reflects your personality to a degree. So, something as individual as your handwriting should surely reveal an enormous amount. The term 'graphology' (estimating character from handwriting) was coined by the Frenchman Jean Michon who, after years of study, published his findings in a book in 1872. Modern graphologists take into account such features as legibility, pressure, slant, size, spacing and layout as well as the characteristics of the upper, middle and lower zones of the handwriting. The upper zone is supposed to relate to the intellect, the middle zone to the emotions and the lower zone to the instincts. It sounds plausible.

But a study by the British Columbia Civil Liberties Association concluded that graphologists score no higher than chance when it comes to assessing personality traits. Why, then, do so many people believe in it? It's the Forer Effect again (see earlier in this chapter).

There *are* a few things you can tell from handwriting (that somebody is physically weak, has poor co-ordination, or is unskilled in the visual arts, for example) but you can tell very little about whether or not someone scores high or low for the Big Five personality traits.

> **Insight**
> Those who examine handwriting to check for authenticity and fraud are known as forensic document examiners and are a different case.

Self-coaching tip

The very fact that other people think they can tell important things about you from your handwriting is good reason to pay attention to it. Here's a quick round-up of the handwriting styles that are said to be associated with the Big Five traits:

- ▶ High Openness – wide left margin; curled endings on various letters; top loop of initial letter inflated.
- ▶ Low Openness – low loops or no loops in the lower zone; vertical angular writing with heavy pressure; dominant lower zone.
- ▶ High Conscientiousness – small, even writing.
- ▶ Low Conscientiousness – missing i dots and t bars; disconnected letters; widening left margin; illegible signature.
- ▶ High Extroversion – large initial letters; brightly coloured ink; right slant; narrow right margin; right extension of end strokes.
- ▶ Low Extroversion – upright or left slant; light pressure; large distance between words.
- ▶ High Agreeableness – right slant; wide even loops; symmetry.
- ▶ Low Agreeableness – large letters; heavy pressure; narrow writing
- ▶ High Neuroticism – irregular letter size, pressure and spacing; downward-sloping lines.
- ▶ Low Neuroticism – regular, rhythmic handwriting.

Past lives

Morey Bernstein sold farm and mining equipment for a living and hypnotized people for fun in his spare time. One day in 1952 he hypnotized housewife Virginia Tighe in his hometown of Pueblo, Colorado, and gave a whole new impetus to Western ideas of reincarnation. Under hypnosis, Virginia spoke with an Irish accent and said she had lived in Cork, Ireland, in the nineteenth century with the name Bridey Murphy. In the sessions that followed she sang Irish songs, told Irish stories and described more and more of her life, including her burial in Belfast in 1864. Bernstein wrote a book called *The Search For Bridey Murphy* which caused a sensation and became a best-seller.

There are obvious attractions to a belief in past lives. If there are past lives, then there's life after death. But they would also account for child prodigies as well as those maddening personality traits for which there seems to be no precedent in the family.

How could Mrs Tighe have known so much about Ireland in the nineteenth century? It turned out that she didn't know quite so much after all. Journalists checking things out in Ireland couldn't find any confirmation that any such person ever existed. The explanation was closer to home. In the first place, Virginia's parents were of Irish extraction, a fact not mentioned in the book. But the really crushing discovery was made by a reporter for the *Chicago American*. Opposite the house in which Virginia had grown up, there had lived a woman called Bridie Murphy Corkell. Virginia's recovered memories were not of a past life but from her childhood.

Psychologist Robert Baker carried out an interesting experiment on past life regression. He divided some 60 students into three groups. Those in Group A were told they were about to experience an exciting new therapy that would help them uncover their past lives. Those in Group B were told they were about to learn about a therapy that might or might not bring back memories of previous lives. Those in Group C were told that the therapy was crazy and that normal people did not experience past lives. All the subjects were then hypnotized and taken back to their 'past lives'.

Here are the results:
▶ Group A: 85% 'remembered' past lives.
▶ Group B: 60% 'remembered' past lives.
▶ Group C: 10% 'remembered' past lives.

The results don't prove that people don't have previous lives but they do prove that belief in past lives is highly suggestible. Meanwhile, those who do believe in past lives still have no hard evidence.

The enneagram

In his book *In Search Of The Miraculous*, P. D. Ouspensky, the follower of the Russian mystic G. I. Gurdjieff (1877–1949), wrote that 'All knowledge can be included in the enneagram and with the help of the enneagram it can be it can be interpreted.' That allegedly includes the decoding of the personality.

The enneagram is certainly a lot of fun if you find mathematical quirks intriguing. It is a circle with nine equidistant points marked on the circumference and numbered 1 to 9 in clockwise order. The main quirk is that if you divide 1 by 7 you get the sequence 142857 repeated infinitely. Straight lines are accordingly drawn across the circle from 1 to 4 to 2 to 8 to 5 to 7 and back to 1. The other quirk is that if you divide 1 by 3 you get an infinite series of threes. The remaining numbers are all multiples of three (3, 6 and 9) and are linked by a second set of straight lines to create an equilateral triangle.

The nine points represent nine basic traits and the way they link through the 'magic numbers' is supposed to portray the full complexity of your personality.

More recently, Oscar Ichazo (b. 1931) devised a system called Arica, which he named after the city in Chile where he opened his first school in 1971. The Arica system, he says, observes that the human body and psyche is composed of nine independent but interconnected systems. Ichazo claims that Arica, based on enneagons (nine-sided figures) is 'scientific' whereas other authors working with enneagrams are 'unscientific'.

Enneagrams have become popular in recent years. As we saw in Chapter 1, the human personality can certainly be broken down into nine basic traits, but it can equally be described in 16 or five or any other number you care to mention. There's no scientific evidence that nine reflects any special properties.

10 TIPS FOR SUCCESS

1 Phrenology doesn't work.

2 Projective personality tests are less reliable than self-reporting tests.

3 Belief in astrology is explained by the Forer Effect.

4 Birth order has very little proven impact on personality.

5 However, birth order may have a slight impact on sexual orientation.

6 The relative length of the second and fourth fingers of your right hand is a reflection of your androgen exposure in the womb.

7 Graphology provides very little information about personality.

8 Belief in past life regression is highly suggestible.

9 There is no scientific evidence that anybody has lived before and therefore no evidence that past lives can affect personality.

10 There is no scientific evidence that the enneagram is a useful tool in uncovering human personality.

5

Financial success

In this chapter you will learn:
- *how materialistic you are*
- *how likely you are to become rich*
- *how to use your personality to be more successful.*

Researchers at the University of Bonn, Germany, asked 101 men
and women to play a computer gambling game. They were told they
could, if they wished, donate any winnings to a poor child in Peru.
Given that it was only a game involving small sums, you might think
that all affluent Westerners would donate their entire winnings. But it
didn't work out that way. Some of the players were far more desperate
than others not only to make money but also to hang on to it.

Here's a very intriguing thing. We all carry a gene called catechol-
O-methyl transferase, or COMT for short. COMT comes in two
versions, G and A. It turns out that among the players, more than a
fifth of those with the G version gave away all their winnings. But of
those who carried the A version only 2 per cent did the same.

We'll be taking a look at the connection between personality and
genes in Chapter 10. For now we're just interested in the fact that
some people are naturally very much more materialistic than others.
Which are you?

Do you sincerely want to be rich?

Back in the 1950s and 1960s a financial products entrepreneur would
vet potential sales recruits by asking them a simple question: 'Do you
sincerely want to be rich?' Bernie Cornfeld became almost as famous
for that phrase as for the eventual and spectacular crash of his multi-
billion dollar company, Investors Overseas Services.

It may have seemed like a stupid question. Who wouldn't want to be rich? But the answer may surprise you. Most people.

You see, people *say* they'd like to be rich but only a very small proportion really try. Yes, of course, you'd happily accept the money if someone gave it to you. But are you really willing to exert yourself to *make* money. You may say you want to be wealthy. You may believe it. That is, your conscious mind wants to be rich, but what about your unconscious? Why on Earth, you might ask, would your unconscious *not* want you to be wealthy? Well, here are some possible reasons and they might surprise you:

▶ You identify yourself as someone who is struggling, not as someone who has arrived.
▶ Life might seem to have no point if you've arrived.
▶ You don't genuinely believe you *could* be very successful.
▶ The stress of trying to succeed might be bad for you.
▶ There are other things you'd unconsciously prefer to devote yourself to.

So let's try to find out not how eager for wealth you say you are, but how determined you really are. Just tick every answer you agree with.

1 I prefer to set or agree to goals I know I can easily achieve, rather than aim for higher goals at which I might fail.
2 I wouldn't like work colleagues to think I considered myself better than them.
3 I don't like to be in competition with other people.
4 I wouldn't want to be promoted to a level at which I had too much responsibility or was under too much pressure.
5 If it's a choice between getting on and having true friends and happiness, I'll go for true friends and happiness.
6 I would prefer to work in a job that fascinates me even though it's poorly paid, rather than take a job that's highly paid but uninteresting.
7 I'd like to make a million and then I'd retire.
8 When I get a bonus or windfall, I spend it enjoying myself.
9 It's very important to maintain a work/life balance.
10 Money is only one way of measuring success.
11 If you come second or third in a competition you've also done very well.
12 Just because you're poor, that doesn't make you a loser; you could still be a very interesting person.

13 If you devote yourself to something you genuinely enjoy, and make a good job of it, you will get rich eventually.

14 I prefer to spend money on experiences rather than objects.

15 I recognize that many other people are superior to me.

How to score

For every tick, score 1; for every statement you didn't tick, score 0. The higher your score the less ambitious, competitive, and driven you are. If you scored close to 15, you don't care about money and you're only ever going to get rich by pure chance. If you scored around the middle, you're like the vast majority of people, interested in money but not caring about it sufficiently to make a really serious effort. If you scored close to 0, you're highly materialistic and you therefore meet Bernie Cornfeld's requirement.

Self-coaching tip

Doesn't ticking that statement about earning a million and then retiring demonstrate a burning desire for money? Not at all. Really wealthy people almost never give up, no matter how much they have. Putting a ceiling on wealth is not the act of a person who sincerely wants to be rich.

Beauty and the bank

Here's another 'stupid' question. How attractive are you? You shouldn't be too surprised to be asked, since you've already learned that being attractive is an advantage in more things than sex. And, yes, research shows that being attractive is also an advantage when it comes to wealth.

The fact is that the more attractive you are, the more you're likely to earn. And that doesn't just apply to the obvious things such as acting and modelling. It seems to apply to all kinds of professions. A team of researchers led by Irene Frieze at the University of Pittsburgh devised a five-point scale of attractiveness which was applied to MBA graduates. They found that, on average, men earned $2,600 extra for each additional unit of attractiveness, while women earned $2,150 extra per unit. A similar study of attorneys in the USA found that, five years after graduation, those considered the most attractive were earning more than those considered the least attractive.

It's the same story with height. It's well known that women prefer to date tall men. Less well-recognized is that companies prefer to employ tall men and women, and tend to reward them better than their shorter colleagues. It's been calculated that each extra inch is worth around $600 in salary a year. Political candidates tend to get more votes for being tall, making it very difficult to become president of the USA if you're below average height.

And then there's the issue of weight. Economists have calculated that being 65 pounds overweight will cost a woman 7 per cent of the salary she would otherwise have received.

So is all this just a matter of prejudice? Or is there actually some kind of link between attractiveness, height, weight, and ability? Well, there *could* be. In order to be considered attractive, you need (among other things) to be symmetrical. And being symmetrical is a marker for 'good genes' and intelligence. In the same way, tallness is also a marker for genetic fitness.

However, if you're not tall, thin or considered attractive, don't despair. All of this research deals in averages. There's nothing to say individuals can't beat the odds. And, of course, many do. In fact, quite a lot of people are driven to compensate for disadvantages and end up being more successful than those to whom fate dealt a good hand.

Self-coaching tip

In one experiment, people consulting a psychiatrist were deliberately made to wait while the psychiatrist took a telephone call. People considered attractive waited on average three minutes and twenty seconds before interrupting. People considered unattractive waited an average of nine minutes. That's already interesting. But even more interesting is that both the 'attractive' and the 'unattractive' considered themselves assertive. If you want to get rich, don't delude yourself. Make sure you're up there with the genuinely assertive group.

Brains and the bank

Although every schoolchild can point to men and women who became rich despite leaving 'boring' education at a young age and without qualifications, numerous studies show that, on average, one year of education raises lifetime earnings by around 5 per cent One study found that high processing speed and numerical ability were each associated with roughly a 9 per cent increase in lifetime earnings.

But earning an extra few thousand a year is hardly the same thing as getting rich. That generally tends to require a special kind of intelligence known as lateral thinking. That's the ability to 'think out of the box', to spot opportunities that others have missed and to identify new trends almost before they've begun.

Here are some questions designed to test you lateral thinking ability. Have a go:

1 What can you hold in your right hand but not in your left?
2 If you have two coins totalling 11p and one of them is not a penny, what are the two coins?
3 If you had been a passenger on a long-haul flight to Australia and, by chance, you met the captain in the hotel bar wearing a dress, what would you do?
4 A woman lives on the tenth floor of a block of flats. Every morning she takes the lift down to the ground floor and goes to work. In the evening, if there is someone else in the lift she goes back to her floor directly. Otherwise, she goes to the eighth floor and walks up two flights. How do you account for this?
5 A man built a square house with each side facing south. How is that possible?
6 Is it legal for a man to marry his widow's sister?
7 In cubic centimetres, how much soil is there in a hole measuring 3m × 2m × 2m?

You'll find the answers to these questions at the end of the chapter. When you read them you may congratulate yourself on your lateral thinking ability. Or you may find yourself tossing this book across the room in exasperation. Don't blame me. I didn't devise them. At least two of them are tests more of 'close reading' than anything else – that's to say, if you're not paying attention you'll misunderstand the question and get the answer wrong.

But, of course, lateral thinking ability on its own is not enough. Let's see what else is needed.

The Big Five and the bank

In Chapter 1 you discovered your Big Five scores. Now, thanks largely to the teachings of Warren Buffet, one of the world's richest self-made men, and to research by Angela Lee Duckworth and David R. Weir at the University of Michigan Retirement Research Center (using data from the Health and Retirement Study (HRS) and the Social Security Administration) we can see what they mean in terms of money.

OPENNESS

One of Buffet's sayings is that if you do what average people do, you'll be average. In order to get rich you must be willing to be different. That argues for high Openness. High Openness is also associated with cognitive efficiency in the frontal lobes of the brain which, in turn, is associated with intelligence. On the other hand, extreme Openness tends to be associated with the pursuit of the mystical rather than the material. So a good dollop of Openness, but not too much.

CONSCIENTIOUSNESS

This is the big one in terms of wealth creation. Duckworth and Weir concluded that, in technical terms, a one standard deviation increase in Conscientiousness is associated with a 9 per cent increase in lifetime earnings (which translated as $1,500 a year). In non-technical terms, the more Conscientious you are, the higher your lifetime earnings.

As for Buffet, five of his key rules translate as high Conscientiousness. Here they are:

▶ **Reinvest your profits.** It's part of Buffet folklore that, as a youngster, he and a friend bought a second-hand pinball machine and put it in a barbershop. With the profits they bought more machines and created a nice little business. Or to put it another way, don't give in to the impulse to spend the profits on having a good time.

▶ **Know when to quit.** Psychologists have devised a game known as the Iowa Gambling Task. In a nutshell, there are four decks of cards. Two of them (call them A and B) offer the opportunity to win big rewards but with the risk of big losses. The two others (call them C and D) offer small rewards and small losses. After playing the game for a while it becomes apparent that the losses on A and B always exceed any winnings, while the losses on C and D are always less than any winnings. Nevertheless some people, those who are low in Conscientiousness, just can't stop themselves going for packs A and B. Not good in business, as Warren knows very well.

▶ **Be persistent.** This advice seems at first sight to contradict the adage of 'know when to quit'. But it's all a question of judgement. Nothing comes easy and if you're still sure that you're right, then you must keep on. One of Buffet's most famous sayings is that the stock market (which is where he made most of his money) is a mechanism for transferring wealth from the impatient to the patient – that's to say, from people low in Conscientiousness to people high in Conscientiousness.

▶ **Assess the risks.** And how exactly do you make those all important judgements? A highly useful tool is upside/downside. If the money you might make on the upside is substantially in excess of any losses you might make on the downside, then (assuming other factors are also positive) you go ahead. This is a mindset that can be applied to all kinds of things, not just money-making.

▶ **Watch small expenses.** They have a way of adding up to a lot of money. Buffet is noted for his frugality. He doesn't employ a chauffeur and lives in the same house he bought in 1958, today valued at around $700,000. (However, in 1989 he did succumb to a private jet.)

Nevertheless, there's also one rule that's more consistent with low Conscientiousness:

▶ **Never suck your thumb.** That's Buffet-speak for 'don't procrastinate'. When the terms of a deal are right, do it. People low in Conscientiousness find it easy to make quick decisions, people high in Conscientiousness like to mull things over – sometimes too long.

EXTROVERSION

Duckworth and Weir found no correlation between Extroversion and wealth, one way or the other. Nor does Buffet seem to have anything to say on the matter, either directly or indirectly.

AGREEABLENESS

Duckworth and Weir found that in the study of *couples*, high Agreeableness tended to be associated with lower wealth. According to the Washington-based Institute for Policy Studies (IPS), the Chief Executive Officers (CEOs) of the 50 companies that laid off the most workers in the wake of the 2007 subprime crisis took home 42 per cent more pay than their peers on the Standard & Poor's 500 index. So ruthlessness, which is associated with low Agreeableness, appears to pay off.

Buffet seems to agree. His advice is:

▶ **Spell out the deal before you start.** Another piece of the Buffet folklore is that he once did some work for his grandfather, clearing snow after a blizzard, and at the end of it received only a few cents. The young Buffet resolved that in future every detail of a contract must be clearly agreed before anything is done. Or, to put it another way, he would never trust anyone again to do the decent thing, a characteristic of those who are low in Agreeableness.

Against that, Buffet also said that real success is being able to do good things and being loved by people you want to be loved by. But, then, that was Buffet in old age, having already amassed one of the greatest fortunes in the world. A more compelling argument in terms of wealth creation is that co-operation (requiring high Agreeableness) can be a very successful strategy (see Chapter 8).

NEUROTICISM

Duckworth and Weir concluded that, in technical terms, a one standard deviation increase in emotional stability is associated with a 5 per cent increase in lifetime earnings (which translated as $700 a year). In non-technical terms, the lower you are in Neuroticism, the higher your lifetime earnings.

Against that, psychologists Barrick and Mount found that men and women who scored above average for Neuroticism tended to be more successful in professional occupations.

And Buffet's adjudication? He comes down on the side of higher Neuroticism:

▶ **Limit what you borrow.** Buffet claims never to have borrowed any significant sum. On the other hand, it's in the nature of his business that he looks after money on behalf of others which, it could be argued, is an oblique way of borrowing. A fear of being in debt is consistent with high Neuroticism, but Buffet also sees it as good business.

Two other Buffet rules, already mentioned, 'watch small expenses' and 'spell out the deal before you start' are also consistent with high Neuroticism.

So, what's best? The key is probably in that phrase 'emotional stability'. Higher than average Neuroticism translates into sound business practices, and a greater fear of failure that increases motivation and hard work. But it should never be so high that emotional stability is threatened.

Self-coaching tip

For years, Warren Buffet (born 1930) has been one of the top ten richest men in the world. A lot of people think he taught himself, trading shares as a youngster and building his capital up.

But it wasn't quite that easy for him and it won't be quite that easy for you.

The outstanding feature of the Warren Buffet story is the huge amount of preparation that he did. Here is a man who from the time he was a child was always trying one money-making scheme or another. Yes, he bought his first shares at the age of 11. But he also attended the Wharton Business School, the University of Nebraska-Lincoln, the Columbia Business School and the New York Institute of Finance. He worked as an investment salesman, as a securities analyst, and under Benjamin Graham, the legendary 'value investor'.

Here's another thing. If you started with a thousand pounds or dollars and consistently doubled your capital every four years (something no one has ever done), you'd still only have about four million at the end of a normal working life. In Buffet, we're talking about a man who was once worth over $60 *billion*.

Buffet may not like borrowing, but he increased the capital available to him in another way, by investing on behalf of other people and being in charge of their funds. And there have been some difficult times, with quite spectacular losses that had to be absorbed. If Buffet hadn't worked his way into the 'big time' at other people's risk, he wouldn't ever have become seriously rich. If Buffet had applied himself as diligently to, say, delivering mail or taking X-rays, he'd still be seriously poor. If you want to

Employed or self-employed?

One way of earning money at someone else's risk is to get a job. True, people like Bill Gates, Warren Buffet and Lord Sugar all started their own businesses. But you can also get rich as an employee. The total compensation packages for the world's top managers run into the tens of millions each. Very few people with their own businesses will ever earn even 1 per cent of that and many go bankrupt and lose their homes. Deciding which route is best for you is not so much a question of money as of personality. What kind of workstyle suits you?

My workstyle is very different to most people's. I frequently put in seven-day weeks and am often at my desk late at night. But when the mood comes over me I can just take off. I can be on the beach in half an hour and stay as long as I like. Or I can be on the ski slopes in two. I almost always work Saturdays and Sundays so that I can take time off when things are less crowded. And I need no one's permission but my own. Best of all, I can work from my home in Spain, using the internet. I think my workstyle is great, but there are those who feel sorry for me, sitting long hours alone in front of my computer. They, by contrast, relish interacting with other people and having work colleagues to banter with. Will I ever be rich? What do you think? But some authors are.

Here are some questions to ask yourself about workstyle:

1 Do I prefer to be given specific tasks or to work on my own initiative?
2 Do I need the security of a regular salary or can I live with an erratic income?
3 Am I willing to commute or would I prefer something local?
4 Am I willing to be away from home from time to time?

5 Am I willing to accept set hours or would I prefer the freedom to choose?

6 Do I prefer to work on my own or as part of a team?

7 Do I prefer to work for a big, important company or a small, family-owned company, or for myself?

8 Am I happy to work every day in the same place or would I prefer variety?

9 Am I happy to wear formal clothing or do I prefer to dress casually?

10 Do I like to interact with lots of different people every day or do I prefer to work alone?

11 Am I willing to take risks with my own money and even my own home?

12 How good am I at handling stress?

There are no right or wrong answers. It's simply a question of knowing yourself and becoming a round peg in a round hole. Don't be afraid to try lots of different things. You can't always predict in advance how you'll feel.

And now here are the answers to that test of lateral thinking:

1 Your left hand.

2 One of them is not a penny but the other one could be – the answer is 1p and 10p.

3 Most people immediately imagine a cross-dressing man but, of course, women can also be pilots.

4 The woman is too short to reach the button for the tenth floor.

5 The house was built at the north pole.

6 It's impossible because for his wife to be a widow, he'd have to be dead.

7 There's no soil in the hole because...it's a hole.

10 TIPS FOR SUCCESS

1 Some people are naturally more materialistic than others.

2 There's a huge difference between wanting to be rich and really trying to be rich.

3 Attractive people have an advantage.

4 Mum and Dad were right – the better educated you are, the wealthier you're likely to become.

5 It's not just IQ that counts; lateral thinking ability is important, too.

6 Of the Big Five personality traits, high Conscientiousness is the most closely associated with wealth creation.

7 Other useful personality traits for the pursuit of wealth are: above average Openness, lower than average Agreeableness and enough Neuroticism to keep you motivated.

8 If you sincerely want to be rich, you need to do a lot of homework.

9 If you want to make big money, you have to position yourself where there is big money to be made.

10 Whatever you do, try to find a workstyle that suits your personality.

How rational are you?

In this chapter you will learn:
- *how things may not always be as simple as they seem*
- *how to understand odds*
- *that you may not be quite as rational as you thought.*

When it comes to our personalities, we don't all want the same things. But there's one quality that just about everybody desires and believes they have. They, you and I all want to be rational.

But are we?

Are *you*?

The three card test

Let's kick off with something fairly straightforward. I have three cards. One of the cards has two white faces (sides), another has two red faces and the third has one white face and one red face. While you are looking away I place one of the cards on the table. On turning back, you see that it has a red face upwards. I now ask you what is the probability that it is the card with two red faces.

Give your answer before reading on.

I suspect you reasoned like this. 'It cannot possibly be the card with two white faces, therefore it is either the card with two red faces, or the card with one of each. Since it's a choice between two cards, the probability must be one in two.'

If you did reason that way, you were wrong. In fact, there aren't two possibilities but *three*. You could be seeing the red face of the red and white card, or one of two faces of the all red card. Of these three possibilities, in two cases the hidden face would be red and in only one case would it be white. So it's more likely than not that the hidden face is red and the probability would be expressed as two in three.

Take a little time to think about it because we're going to move on to something a little more fiendish, this time involving not three cards but three boxes. It's known as the Monty Hall problem after the presenter of the American game show *Let's Make A Deal*.

The Monty Hall problem

On a table are three identical boxes with lids. While you're out of the room, I place money in one of the boxes, then close all the lids. I know where the money is but you don't. I call you back and invite you to guess where the money is – if you're right, you win it. Once you've made your choice I open not your box but another one that is empty (since I know where the money is I also know which box is empty). I now offer you the possibility of remaining with your original selection or of switching to the other closed box. You make your decision, win the money or not, leave the room and I start the game all over again.

Now here's the big question. Is it better to stick with your original box or to switch? Or doesn't it matter?

Think about it for a bit.

Most people would probably reason that there are two boxes left and since one of them must contain the money, the probability works out at one in two.

If you also thought that, then you were thinking irrationally. But it's going to be difficult to make you believe it.

You see, when you were confronted with the three closed boxes, the one you chose had a one-third chance of being the box with the money. The other two boxes *together* had a two-thirds chance. When I opened one of the two, showing it to be empty, the other *on its own* now inherited the two-thirds probability. So by switching you would increase the probability of winning from one-third to two-thirds.

So the correct strategy in this case is: *always* switch.

Not convinced? Here's another way of looking at it.

Let's suppose your original choice was correct. In that case you will lose out by switching. But if your original choice was wrong, you'll win by switching. Now, here's the clever bit. On average, your original choice will be correct on only one of three occasions, but incorrect on two out of three occasions. Therefore you must improve your winnings by following the strategy of always switching.

Still not convinced? Then play the game with a friend. Try it, say, 50 times switching and 50 times not switching and compare the results.

Examining the evidence

Here's a standard exercise. I give you the sequence of numbers: 2, 4, 6. I tell you it obeys a certain rule and that you have to discover the rule by putting forward other sequences of three numbers. I will tell you if the new sequences are consistent with the rule or not. When you're confident you know the rule, you announce it and I'll tell you if you're right or wrong. If you're wrong, you carry on selecting more triplets until you eventually succeed.

Most people propose, say, 8, 10, 12 and then, maybe, something like 26, 28, 30. I say the sequences are consistent and they then announce: 'Even numbers ascending by two.' I tell them they're wrong. Then they might propose, say, 9, 11, 13 on the basis of: 'Any three numbers ascending by two.' Also wrong.

It's interesting how many people fail to work out the rule, but even more interesting how many refuse to abandon an incorrect hypothesis, simply restating it in different words when they're told they're wrong.

In fact, the rule is: 'Any three numbers in ascending order.' Of course, you can't have worked that out on the basis of what I've told you (you would have needed to take part in the experiment). There are two reasons people who actually are in the experiment most often fail to get the rule. The first is that it's too simple and they're looking for something more ingenious.

But the other, more important reason, is that we all tend to look for evidence that confirms a supposition, rather than looking for evidence that contradicts a supposition. That's why most people's first proposed sequence is something like '8, 10, 12' (confirming the 'even numbers ascending by two supposition') rather than, say, '10, 15, 20' (contradicting the supposition).

> ### Self-coaching tip
>
> When you want to check a hypothesis, do your best to *disprove* it, not prove it.

The publishing sting

We've all suffered the rejection of some project or other – perhaps a thesis, an article submitted to a magazine, a business plan submitted to a bank, or a design of some kind. But have you ever been in the position of making the decision to accept or reject? And, if so, were you really rational about it?

All kinds of experiments have shown that, in fact, such judgements seldom are entirely rational. Whenever there's a quiet news period, newspapers are rather fond of carrying out stings to prove how irrational critics, art galleries, publishers, agents and the like really are. In 2006, the *Sunday Times* did just that, submitting typed manuscripts of the opening chapters of works by V. S. Naipaul, a Nobel prize winner, and the respected but less well-known Stanley Middleton, to 20 publishers and agents. There was only one expression of interest.

In another sting, Jerzy Kosinsky's novel *Steps*, which had won the American National Book Award, was typed out in manuscript form and sent to 27 agents and publishers under a new, unknown name. None recognized it and all rejected it.

Ah yes, you might say, but these are commercial decisions based on the author's fame or lack of it, not literary merit. And the case of best-selling novelist Doris Lessing suggests that might be the case. As an experiment, she herself submitted a novel to her own long-time publishers under an assumed name. What happened? It was rejected.

But surely the same thinking wouldn't apply where scientific merit rather than commercial potential was the yardstick? Well, let's see what happened when articles that had previously been published by various prestigious psychology journals were resubmitted some time later. But this time the names of the genuine authors – all leading psychologists and all from famous universities – were removed and replaced with unknown names. Of the 12 journals subject to the sting, one agreed to publish, three spotted that the article had been published before, and eight rejected on the grounds that the editors, and the referees, did not consider that the articles merited publication.

And that's the key point. The editors and referees were supposed to be making decisions based on rational assessments of the scientific merit. Instead, they based them on the lack of prestige of the apparent authors, without regard to the content.

Self-coaching tip

When submitting any project for approval, always pay attention to the psychological factors that aren't supposed to be relevant but, in reality, are – such as presentation, references, endorsements and so on.

The sunk cost error

Have you ever said, or thought, anything like this:

- ▶ We've gone too far to turn back.
- ▶ It would be a complete waste of 20 years if we split up.
- ▶ I've invested too much money in this to stop.

These are all examples of what's known as the 'sunk cost error'. That's to say, rather than select a course of action based on the facts as they are now, you continue with the present policy, entirely because of the time, money or emotion that you've sunk into it already.

Wars are full of sunk cost errors: 'To stop now would mean those who have sacrificed their lives will have died for nothing.' So, even more people die. In the First World War trenches, it soon became apparent that, on average, attackers suffered more casualties than defenders. Yet General Haig continued to order men to go 'over the top'. In just a few hours, as many as 50,000 men would die. The madness could not be stopped because to do so would mean admitting that men had 'died for nothing'.

The consequences error

Imagine you're the judge at the trial of a motorist who, while driving too fast, lost control of his car in a crowded high street, causing it to smash into a shop window and break the glass. What kind of sentence do you think that merits? Decide before reading on.

Now imagine a new case is brought before you. This time, it's a motorist who, while driving too fast, lost control of his car in a crowded high street, causing it to smash into a group of pedestrians, one of whom was killed. What sentence would you consider appropriate in this case?

If, in fact, you favoured a harsher sentence for the latter case than the first one, are you really being rational? After all, the motorists' failings were exactly the same in both cases. The *consequences* were different but they were outside the control of those motorists. Whether or not pedestrians were killed was down to chance – the street was crowded on both occasions. Logically, the sentence should be the same in both cases. In the real world, it seldom is because most people, including politicians and judges, are not always logical.

In an experiment that has become a classic, volunteers were shown a video of a car accident. Some of the volunteers were then asked, 'How fast were the cars going when they smashed into each other?' The other volunteers were asked, 'How fast were the cars going when they hit one another?' The first group gave an average estimate of 41 miles an hour, while for the second group the figure was 34 miles an hour. The difference was entirely down to the choice of language in putting two questions which, nevertheless, had identical meanings.

Would you succumb to that kind of thing? Most people do.

The anchoring error

If you ever give to charity online, you may have noticed that, quite often, you're invited to select one of half a dozen predetermined donations. There's also usually a button for 'other'. Let's say all the predetermined options are well above the sum you'd been intending, do you click on 'other' and donate your original choice, or do you select the smallest of the given options? Obviously the charities find they can bump up the average donation in this way.

This is related to an effect called anchoring. Anchoring is the phenomenon by which, unless they know the answer, people tend to select numbers that are close to (or 'anchored on') any number they were first presented with. In cultures where haggling over price is common, salesmen understand anchoring very well. On holiday, you visit shops in the medina to buy a rug. In one you find something you particularly like. The salesman quotes you 1,000 units of the local currency. You had been thinking of 300 but, now that a price of 1,000 has been given, you focus your attention on getting a 'reasonable' discount and finally settle on 900. The figure of 1,000 'anchored' you in that zone, making it difficult for you to contemplate offering anything very much lower.

When people are given a series of numbers, the anchoring effect means they tend to opt for something in the middle. For example, I ask you how many times a week you engage in a certain activity. If I present you with this scale:

0   1–3   4–6   7–10   11–15

I'll almost certainly get a lower average score than if I present you with this one:

0–5   6–10   11–15   16–20   over 20

Or I ask you your view on the present government:

Very dissatisfied	Dissatisfied	Neither dissatisfied nor satisfied	Satisfied

There will be a tendency towards selecting either 'Dissatisfied' or 'Neither dissatisfied nor satisfied' so as not to seem too extreme. So if I present my poll a little differently, I'm likely to get a better result for the government:

Dissatisfied	Satisfied	Very satisfied	Extremely satisfied

Now the government can claim a high proportion of people who are either 'Satisfied' or 'Very satisfied'.

> ### Self-coaching tip
>
> When someone tries to 'anchor' you to a number, ignore it and make your own judgement quite independently. On the other hand, when you're trying to persuade others, try to 'anchor' them. In experiments, even mentioning a number that had nothing to do with the subject under discussion had an influence on people.

The percentages problem

Let's say you're selecting your choice of contraceptive. You're told that for the Pill it's 99 per cent effective. Well, in the real world, it doesn't come much better than that, does it? You can use the Pill all your reproductive life and, unless you're incredibly unlucky, you'll never get pregnant by mistake!

How would you rate the chance of you or your partner, using the Pill correctly, ever getting pregnant? Give your answer before reading on.

In the case of the Pill, what does this 99 per cent figure actually relate to? It means that if 100 women use the Pill *for a year*, one of them *will* become pregnant. And that's just one year. On that basis, well over one-third of women on the Pill who are sexually active throughout their reproductive years will get pregnant at some point. Not quite so reassuring after all.

> ### Self-coaching tip
>
> When people quote odds, it's very important to pin down exactly what they mean.

The base rate problem

Let's say you're responsible for security in your company. You're having a problem with theft by staff. A salesman tells you he can supply a lie detector that has an accuracy of 90 per cent. It sounds great. Out of every ten guilty employees, nine will be caught by the lie detector and only one will get away with it.

Would you use the lie detector? Give your answer before reading on.

There's an often overlooked problem here. If you knew who the guilty staff were you wouldn't need the lie detector. You're going to be obliged to test everyone. Let's say there are 1,000 employees and 5 per cent (50 people) are stealing. When you test those 50 people you will catch 45. But you'll also be testing 950 innocent people and, of those, 95 will be pronounced guilty in error.

Now the figures don't look so good at all. For every guilty person you catch, you're going to condemn two innocent people.

This is what's known as the 'base rate' problem. Here it is in its most infuriating form. Don't say you haven't been forewarned.

Late one wet winter's afternoon, a woman hears the screech of tyres and on looking out of her window sees that a taxi has knocked over a cyclist and sped away. She phones the emergency services. When interviewed by the police, she states confidently that it was a red taxi. In fact, two taxi companies operate in the town. There's a fleet of 15 with red paintwork, while the more successful yellow cabs comprise a fleet of 85 vehicles. The police decide to test the woman's eyesight in the same gloomy conditions as the day of the accident and find that she correctly distinguishes red cabs 80 per cent of the time.

Here's the big question. Was the cab that actually knocked over the cyclist more likely to be red or yellow?

Think about it before reading on.

Well, the woman said it was a red cab and she was proven to be right 80 per cent of the time. So, in all probability it was a red cab. Wasn't it? Actually, no. Just as in the example of the lie detector, it's essential to consider the base rate. It's true that the probability of the woman having seen a yellow cab and mistakenly having thought it was red is just .2 (remember, she was right 80 per cent of the time). But we also have to take into account the probability of any cab having been a yellow cab, and that was .85 (remember, of the 100 cabs in the town 85 are yellow). Multiplying the two figures together we find the probability of her having seen a yellow cab and having thought it was red is .17. But, applying the same rationale, the probability of her having seen a red cab and having thought it was red is .15 × .8, which is a much lower figure of .12. So the cab involved in the accident was more likely to have been yellow than red.

> ### Self-coaching tip
>
> You must take the base rate into account whenever you're trying to assess the likelihood of something.

Configural reasoning

Human beings are very good at what's known as serial or sequential processing of data. That's to say, they can progress from point to point in a logical, linear manner. Many of the problems we have to deal with require this kind of thinking. However, there are other kinds of problems that require the ability to take various interconnected factors into account simultaneously, not one after the other. This is known as configural reasoning and human beings are not very good at it. It tends to boggle our minds. We just can't cope with too much data all at once. That's why you'll often hear people say things like 'Let's just cut to the bottom line' or 'Just give me the conclusion'.

It's difficult to process all that interacting data, so there's a tendency to try to rejig problems in such a way that 'linear' thinking can be applied.

There are all kinds of examples in medicine where combinations of symptoms need to be evaluated to give an accurate diagnosis. Instead, medical personnel have been known to fall back on adding up the number of symptoms (serial processing).

In one experiment back in the 1930s when tonsillectomies were commonplace, doctors in New York were asked to examine one thousand children. They found that 61 per cent needed their tonsils removed. The remaining children, who hadn't been selected for tonsillectomies, were examined by a second group of doctors who, nevertheless, proclaimed that 45 per cent needed their tonsils removed. The remaining children were examined by a third set of doctors who proclaimed that 46 per cent needed their tonsils removed. And even after that, a fourth set of doctors proclaimed that 45 per cent of the 'survivors' needed tonsillectomies. By the end of the 'fourth round' only 6.5 per cent of children were said not to require surgery, and, no doubt, if the experiment had continued, there would have been no children with tonsils.

Various studies show that the more information people have, the more confident they feel about their judgements and forecasts. And yet, accuracy does not increase. In one study, clinical psychologists rated the accuracy of their own diagnoses at 90 per cent when, in fact, it was 40 per cent. Those betting on horse racing were no more successful when they had a lot of information about the horses, jockeys and racecourses than when they had only a little.

The fact is that most of us can't actually process a large amount of information so, after gaining a general impression, we tend to cling to a small number of facts that support the hypothesis we already have in mind. In the case of the tonsillectomies, New York doctors in the 1930s seem to have worked on the hypothesis that roughly one in two children needed the operation.

> ### Insight
> We tend to take a shortcut by applying simple rules or what psychologists call *heuristics*. We use heuristics all the time and they can be extremely useful. But other heuristics are just daft, including such things as 'Never trust a man who doesn't drink' or 'Never trust a man with a beard' or 'All blondes are stupid'.

The stock market should be so easy. All you have to do is decide if a share will go up in price or go down. How could you go wrong? And yet, large numbers of people do. Why? Because it requires configural reasoning. There are just too many factors that can impact the share price (profit, turnover, cash flow, borrowings, earnings growth, price-earnings ratio, taxation, changes in the law, wars, natural disasters, accidents and so on). Nobody can really cope with that amount of data. Some, therefore, try to reduce the problem to a simple linear formula – for example, buy when the 20-day moving average crosses up through the 50-day moving average. Others heroically do their best to wade through all the data. But, whatever methods are used, most investors, including professionals, are wrong far more often than they're right. (The successful ones generally make money by running their few winning shares and very quickly cutting the losses on their numerous losing shares.)

The problem of illusory correlation

Let's say a medical researcher is trying to work out if a particular symptom is diagnostic of a particular illness. This person obtains the records of 100 sufferers and finds the symptom is present in 95 of them. Case closed. The researcher concludes that the symptom can be used as a reliable diagnostic tool.

But is that right?

If you're not certain, here's a question that may help clarify the situation:

▶ How many patients have ears?

Of course, our researcher has forgotten to compare the frequency of the disease when the symptom is present, with the *absence* of the disease when the symptom is present. The records of 100 people *without* the disease also needed to be obtained. In fact, it's necessary to have four figures to establish whether a correlation is present or not. The figures are:

▶ the frequency with which A and B occur together
▶ the frequency with which A occurs without B
▶ the frequency with which B occurs without A
▶ where relevant, the frequency with which neither A nor B occurs.

There are plenty of everyday examples of this. Do you:

▶ 'know' who is calling when you hear the telephone ring
▶ find you're already thinking of someone when they happen to ring

- ▶ believe in fortune tellers
- ▶ believe your dreams predict the future
- ▶ have feelings of foreboding that turn out to be prescient?

The basic error is always the ignoring of the negative – not counting all those feelings of anxiety that weren't followed by a catastrophe, all those times the telephone rang and it was not the person you thought, all those predictions which didn't turn out to be true. Which brings us rather neatly to belief in the supernatural.

Self-coaching tip

As in the case of the ascending numbers, you need to look for the evidence that appears to *disprove* the apparent correlation. It's only when you take that into account that you can make a balanced judgement.

Belief in the supernatural

Do you believe there's 'something in' astrology (see Chapter 4)? Do you believe telepathic communication is possible? Do you believe certain people can move objects and bend metal with the power of their minds? If you do, then you're certainly not unusual. Surveys show that in the Western world around three-quarters of adults believe in some psychic phenomena. The higher you are in Openness, the more likely it is.

And yet all of these beliefs are irrational. They've been tested by scientists and convincingly disproved. People who claim to have supernatural powers have never been able to produce them under laboratory conditions. James 'The Amazing' Randi, himself a magician, has offered a prize of one million dollars to anyone who can demonstrate paranormal abilities to the satisfaction of an independent panel and no one has won it. That in itself should be proof enough.

Some of the most famous names in the paranormal haven't even dared try to take on Randi's challenge. But there are some that do, suggesting that as well as fooling others, they've even fooled themselves.

In his book *Paranormality*, Professor Richard Wiseman recounts how he assisted in the testing of a British medium called Patricia Putt. Ten volunteers in turn, dressed in black capes and balaclavas to prevent any information being given away by clothing or appearance, sat in a room with Putt while she attempted to make contact with the spirit world. After she had written down what she had discovered, the ten volunteers were asked to read the various accounts and choose the one that most seemed to apply to them.

It had been agreed that if five or more volunteers correctly identified their readings, Putt would pass the test. In fact, not a single one did. According to Professor Wiseman, Putt was genuinely stunned. She really had believed she could contact the dead (often with the help of her Egyptian spirit guide Ankhara).

Given that these kinds of claims are so easily disproved, where do they come from? Obviously, our ancestors didn't have access to the scientific instruments we do now. They were obliged to put anything they couldn't understand into a box called 'supernatural'. Why did the sun travel across the sky? Why was there thunder and lightning? What was the significance of dreams? Why did people die? What happened afterwards?

More perplexing is why people continue to believe in the paranormal today. For one possible explanation, we have to go even further back in time. The very fact that you exist means that all your ancestors were survivors. They had to live long enough to reproduce in a world filled with danger. And the qualities they would have needed then are the very same qualities that you have inherited now. One of the most important is the ability to look for signals in the world around you and work out what they mean.

Your ancestors would have seen a footprint or a dropping and deduced that an animal had passed that way. They would have seen the footprints leading into a thicket, seen branches move and made the prediction that a dangerous animal was about to leap onto them. In other words, they looked for meaning in nature.

And that's exactly what we're doing when we infer some supernatural power. We see a meteor and convince ourselves it's a message of some sort. We endure a tragedy and conclude that we have a role in some piece of other-worldly theatre that's 'bigger than we are' and 'beyond our understanding'. In short, we investigate, find two and two...and make five. In fact, we're particularly likely to resort to a paranormal explanation when it comes to numbers, because, as we've seen, we're sometimes not very good at understanding them.

COINCIDENCES

Here's a question about numbers – registration numbers. How likely is it that, during the course of tomorrow, you'll spot a car with the following plate: BRB 1960 LE?

Think about it and give your answer, in round numbers, before reading on.

What did you estimate? There are a lot of cars in the world, so would you say a million to one? Ten million to one? A hundred million to one? Then congratulate me, because I saw that registration number today. Which must make me a very special person.

But hang on, you say. Surely there's some sort of failure of logic here.

And, indeed, there is. We're confusing the probability of something happening to a particular person with the probability of something happening to anybody at all. Yet this is exactly the kind of thinking that people use to justify a belief in the paranormal.

Let's take coincidences. How many people would have to be in a room for it to be more likely than not that two of them share the same birthday?

Think about it and decide on your answer before reading on.

What did you decide? Perhaps 365, the number of days in the year? Perhaps 183 (365 divided by two, plus a bit to make the chance higher than even)? The correct answer is a mere 23. And, in fact, with just 30 people the probability rises to 70 per cent. How can it possibly be? The maths is a bit too complicated for a book like this but you can find the calculation on the internet if you want.

In his book *The Psychology Of The Psychic*, David Marks reports that everyone is exposed to around 18 billion 'pairs of events'. Calculating such a number is somewhat arbitrary but even if you were to cut it in half, it's clear that some spectacular coincidences are absolutely inevitable in a lifetime. No supernatural intervention is necessary. If anything, we should be surprised there aren't more of them.

The immortal personality?

And now for a subject that's a bit more difficult. Do you believe there is some part of you that is forever you? All your life? And maybe even after your body is dead? An immortal personality? A soul?

Rationally, it's becoming more and more difficult to maintain that position. Science has demonstrated that there's no moment when life begins, no moment when a soul is created. One to two days can elapse between the penetration of an egg by a sperm and the emergence of a distinct genome. Sometimes, over the next few days, the embryo can split into two or more. If a soul was created by fertilization, what happens then? We also know that between two-thirds and three-quarters of fertilized eggs do not implant successfully, which would mean that an awful lot of 'souls' are very quickly going wherever souls go.

One way of viewing the soul is as the information-processing activity of the brain. If that's what it is, it's something that develops gradually and, usually, declines gradually. But it's what happens if it declines suddenly that poses the greatest obstacle to the belief in a soul.

The neuropsychologist Paul Broks has recounted several of his cases in his book *Into The Silent Land*. They make it terrifyingly clear that your personality is the all too vulnerable product of your brain and will cease to exist if your brain is damaged in certain ways, for instance:

▶ the man devoid of empathy after a road accident
▶ the man overwhelmed by empathy after falling from a tree
▶ the woman who believed herself to be 39 when, in fact, she was 62
▶ the man who underwent a personality change and walked out on his wife and family after developing a tumour in the orbitofrontal region of the brain
▶ the woman who, after infection with herpes simplex, became terrified of raised voices.

All it takes to wipe you out is, say, a blow to the head, or a leak of blood, and the 'you' that everybody knows is gone forever. Your body looks exactly as it did, but the person 'inhabiting' the body is no longer the same.

Self-coaching tip

Never again practise sports without wearing the appropriate head protection.

So how rational were you?

Don't worry if you got a lot of wrong answers. You're no more irrational than anyone else. Most people fail to grasp the right strategies, unless they're trained in statistics and probabilities. In fact, when the solution to the Monty Hall problem was published in *Parade* magazine in 1990, about 10,000 readers wrote in to say the 'always switch' solution was wrong. But it isn't.

10 TIPS FOR SUCCESS

1 Test a hypothesis by setting out to disprove it, not prove it.

2 When submitting a project, pay attention to psychological factors.

3 Make decisions on the basis of the facts now – avoid the 'sunk cost' error.

4 Don't fall for the 'anchoring' trick – but employ the 'anchoring' trick when you want to get your way.

5 Be sure to take the 'base rate' into account when assessing probabilities.

6 It's necessary to have four figures to establish whether there's a correlation or not.

7 Human beings are good at serial processing but not at configural reasoning.

8 No one has ever demonstrated paranormal abilities under strict laboratory conditions.

9 Your soul is probably the information-processing ability of your brain.

10 If you want to make more rational judgements, take a course in statistics and probabilities.

7

Creative success

In this chapter you will learn:
- *how good you are at divergent thinking*
- *how to engage the right side of your brain*
- *how to develop your creativity.*

In a moment we'll find out how creative you are. Then we'll see what you can do to increase your creativity.

If you're thinking that you're not particularly interested in being creative, then you should be. It's not all to do with long hair, crazy ideas and unconventional lifestyles. Businessmen in suits can be creative, scientists in white coats can be creative, engineers in greasy overalls can be creative. And are. The more creative you are, the more successful you're likely to be in anything you do.

Why is there creativity?

Psychologists generally see creativity as an aspect of high Openness, which is characterized by unorthodox ideas, a tendency towards the paranormal, and unconventional behaviour, including a large number of sexual partners.

Indeed, the psychologist Geoffrey Miller has argued that the impulse to be creative is a mating tactic, a way to impress potential partners with the quality of one's mind and therefore one's genes. He cites the bowerbirds of Australia and New Guinea as the Picassos of the avian world. The males construct nests *before* they've found a mate, decorating them with flowers, berries, shells, and even a kind of paint made from regurgitated fruit. The females then assess the nests, like visitors in a gallery, and make their choices.

However, bowerbirds are something of an exception. Most animals do not, as far as anybody can tell, have a creative drive.

But people do. Archaeologists tell us that body painting goes back at least 100,000 years and it's known that the Australian aborigines have been painting on rocks for 50,000 years. In Europe there's evidence for painting, sculpture, jewellery and musical instruments going back at least 35,000 years. So creativity must confer some sort of advantage.

It's true that artistic people tend to have more sexual partners than other people, which fits in with Miller's theory. Byron the poet, Liszt the musician, Warren Beatty the actor, and Augustus John the artist, all fit the bill. But that correlation doesn't prove sex is actually the motive for art. Many famous artists have either been monogamous or had very little sex at all. Salvador Dali, the Surrealist maestro, only had sex with his wife Gala *once*, according to his own account. Van Gogh's sex life wasn't very exciting, nor was that of the poet Robert Browning. And William Blake, the artist and poet of the erotic, so far as anybody knows, only ever had sex with his own wife, although he found her frustratingly inhibited.

And it's *that*, frustration, not sex, that to my mind is at the bottom of the creative impulse. It's down to that well-known phrase, 'Necessity is the mother of invention'. Blake had a necessity to express himself, precisely *because* he was frustrated. His art fulfilled a psychological need. But what about people like Byron and Liszt and so on? How could they have been frustrated? Well, it's all relative. You may be having a lot of sex but you may still have an even higher need. In any case, the number of sexual partners has nothing to do with the amount of sex. One thousand sexual partners could equate to sex once a fortnight with a new partner each time. Nor does it have anything to do with sexual satisfaction. Surveys show that most people are happiest when they have a monogamous relationship.

I would argue that what's needed, along with Openness, is a good serving of Neuroticism. High Neuroticism, you may remember, can be seen as an unusually strong response to negative stimuli. It's associated with words such as anxiety, shame, guilt, sadness and fear – all extremely powerful emotions.

Openness makes creativity possible but it's Neuroticism that, in my opinion, powers it. Happy, contented people just don't feel the urge to change the world, to find new ways of doing things, or to express their innermost feelings. Blake's art was all about the way he wanted his sex life to be. As Wagner wrote to Liszt: 'As I have never in my life known the real and true joy of love, I will raise a monument to that most beautiful of dreams in which, from beginning to end, this love is truly and entirely fulfilled.' That monument was his opera *Tristan and Isolde*.

But it's not only *sexual* frustration that I'm talking about. Any kind of frustration needs to find a solution or an outlet. Anyone who improved a stone axe, or devised a way of sitting on a horse, or directed water into a field, was responding to a frustration and being just as creative as a painter.

Insight

There is a theory that the demand for art is based on its very 'uselessness'. Because it's useless it's the perfect way to advertise wealth. Wealthy people buy hugely expensive watches that don't, in fact, tell the time as accurately as cheap digital watches. They buy diamonds they can't distinguish from glass. And they spend millions on paintings by famous artists while ignoring highly accomplished work by unknown artists. One has only to think of Van Gogh, who was ignored in his lifetime but whose paintings now sell for millions. The difference is that in the nineteenth century, ownership of a Van Gogh conferred no status. Now it does.

How creative are you?

If you scored high in Openness in Chapter 1, then, among other things, you're likely to be unconventional, rebellious, interested in new ideas and, in particular:

▶ good at solving problems requiring 'divergent thinking'.

DIVERGENT THINKING

Joy Paul Guilford (1897–1987) was an American psychologist. Perhaps his interest in the subject came from having parents who gave him a girl's name. In World War Two, he spent a lot of time on the 'Stanines Project', working out why such a high proportion of aircrew trainees weren't graduating, and identified eight different kinds of intellectual abilities that were specific to flying a plane. Later he developed a Structure of Intellect (SIU) theory that involved 150 different abilities. In particular he drew a distinction between what he called 'convergent' thinking and 'divergent' thinking. Convergent thinking is the ability to deduce a single solution to a problem by following rules. Divergent thinking, on the other hand, is the ability to generate multiple solutions to a problem by breaking rules or 'thinking outside the box'.

Ask most people to invent new ways of using an egg cup or a banana and the list will be fairly small. Creative people tend to come up with all kinds of extra possibilities. So let's see how good you are. You have one minute for each of the following tasks:

▶ Think of as many different ways as you can of getting from your kitchen to your bedroom.
▶ Think of as many different ways as you can of wearing a shirt or blouse.
▶ Think of as many different uses as you can for a clothes peg.

Your score
Tally up your number of solutions for the three tasks in total: 10 or under, poor; 11–20, average: 21–30, good; 31 or more, excellent.

The way you use language is another indicator of your divergent thinking abilities. Whenever you think about a word, a lot of related ideas are partially activated in your brain. That's why, if you can't remember someone's name, it helps to think about things associated with that person – their spouse, dog, home and so on. This is known as 'spreading activation'. It's like having parts of your brain on standby. Once your brain knows you're dealing with a particular subject, the relevant memories get 'woken up'.

The point about this is that when creative people are given a word and asked to come up with associated words, they not only think of more answers than other people, but their answers tend to be associated in looser and more inventive ways.

Let's see how you get on with this test. The idea is to find one word that links the other three words in some way (be warned they don't all use the same kind of link):

1 Polish – File – Brush
2 Whip – Dawn – Shot
3 Time – Back – Act

4 Can – Montreal – Snow

5 Alan – Nine – Gut

My answers are at the end of the chapter. But if you came up with different solutions they're fine too. Three solutions, average; four solutions, good; five solutions, excellent.

> **Insight**
>
> Jung used word association to try to understand what was going on in people's unconscious minds. He wasn't just interested in the words chosen but also in the time it took. He believed that a delay indicated some kind of block, possibly because too many words were thrown up and it took time to select one, or, more intriguingly, that a delay indicated the person was uncomfortable with the first word and suppressed it in favour of a safer word. We'll be looking at the unconscious in Chapter 11.

THE TORRANCE TESTS

Building on the work of Guilford, Ellis Paul Torrance (1915–2003) devised his Tests of Creative Thinking in 1966. Originally he tested for fluency, flexibility, originality and elaboration, but he later dropped flexibility as a separate category.

- ▶ **Fluency** – the number of meaningful and relevant ideas generated in response to a stimulus.
- ▶ **Originality** – the rarity of the responses (as demonstrated by statistical analysis).
- ▶ **Elaboration** – the amount of detail.

Here's a little test for you based on one of Torrance's ideas. Copy the motifs below onto three separate sheets of paper and then use them as the starting point for your own artworks.

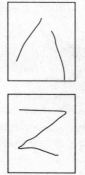

If you were taking the proper test, your drawings would be assessed by a psychologist. Unfortunately, I can't arrange that. The best I can do is tell you the kinds of things the psychologists would be looking for.

If you did something logical or predictable, such as making the two lines into a witch's hat or a shark's fin, then I'm afraid you didn't score very high on creativity. If you felt the urge to add the 'missing' circles then, likewise. Not very creative. But if you did something that no one else was likely to have thought of then you did something creative.

Essentially, you would score marks for the quantity of ideas, originality, imagination, story-telling, ability to convey emotion and humour.

Left brain, right brain

According to Roger Sperry (1913–1994), who won a Nobel prize for his split-brain research, each hemisphere is a system in its own right, to the extent that the two hemispheres could be in conflict. So in a sense we're all two people.

It's the right hemisphere of the brain that's most concerned with visual things and therefore with anything that's visually creative – drawing, painting, sculpting, photography, fashion design and so on.

The left side of the brain is the verbal, rational side that deals with problems serially, using words and numbers. It's something of a simplification to say that the right brain is the exciting, unconventional, hippie you and the left brain the boring, conformist bank manager you. But it's an enjoyably colourful approximation of the truth.

That's why you can feel you're being torn in two directions and can't decide which is the 'real you'. Most of us tend to come down on the side of the left brain, because that's what society wants and what our education system produces. There's a prejudice against the right hemisphere in our society. We tend to think of right-brain people as a bit flaky. Fine if you want someone to paint you a picture but hopeless if you want someone to do something really serious and useful like fill in a tax return.

So if you want to switch on your visual creativity (and your hippie self) you need to switch on the right side of your brain – what Betty Edwards, the acclaimed author of *Drawing on the Right Side of the Brain*, calls R-mode (see Taking it further).

The extent to which one side is dominant can be determined by the Wada Test which involves anaesthetizing one hemisphere. Magnetic resonance imaging and transcranial magnetic stimulation can also help. But we can make a good guess from your behaviour and skills. Here's a little test:

1 When explaining something, do you:
   a. rely largely on words with few gestures
   b. use lots of gestures.
2 Are you usually:
   a. on time for appointments
   b. late for appointments.
3 When making a decision, do you:
   a. weigh the facts carefully
   b. go with your gut feeling.
4 When telling someone what happened, do you:
   a. go through everything in sequence
   b. give the big picture first.
5 Is your desk or work area:
   a. neat and tidy
   b. cluttered.
6 Do you:
   a. prefer things as they are
   b. welcome change.
7 Do you:
   a. do one task at a time
   b. flit backwards and forwards between tasks.
8 If you don't have a watch, do you:
   a. more or less know the time anyway
   b. lose track of time.
9 Are you better at:
   a. remembering names
   b. remembering faces.
10 When you buy a new piece of complicated equipment, do you:
   a. read the instructions carefully
   b. try to have a go straight away.

How did you score?
All the a's are examples of left-brain processing and all the b's are examples of right-brain processing. If you had a lot more a's than b's, you tend to favour your left-brain. If you had a lot more b's than a's, you tend to favour your right-brain. If you scored roughly equal numbers of a's and b's, then you tend to attach equal weight to both hemispheres.

Probably, you were uncertain how to answer some of the questions. Sometimes you tend to respond in one way, sometimes in another. It depends on the circumstances. That only goes to emphasize that no one is entirely left-brain or right-brain. It's more of a preference, of what you feel most comfortable with.

EXPERIENCING THE LEFT–RIGHT SHIFT

Here's an intriguing exercise. Take a look at the drawing. It's a well-known optical-illusion that can be seen as either a vase or as two faces. There's a rather disconcerting moment as the image appears to switch from one to the other. Of course, nothing in the drawing has changed; it's the way you understand the drawing in your brain that changes.

What you're going to do now is make your own version of the drawing. All you need is a piece of paper and a pencil.

1 If you're right-handed, begin by drawing the profile of the face on the left. If you're left-handed, begin in the opposite way by drawing the profile of the face on the right.

2 Draw the horizontal lines that form the top and bottom of the vase.

3 With your pencil, go over the lines of the face two more times, naming them out loud as you do so. Say, 'forehead, nose, upper lip...' and so on.

4 Draw the missing profile.

How did you get on? Probably as you were drawing the missing profile there was a moment when you became confused and didn't know which way to move the pencil. Am I right? In an extreme case, your hand might almost have become paralysed.

If you did get confused, that was probably due to a clumsy switch from the left-brain to the right-brain. At one point you were using the 'verbal' part of your brain, your left-brain (remember the naming of the parts?). Then you switched to the visual side of your brain, your right-brain. That resulted in momentary confusion.

DEVELOPING YOUR RIGHT SIDE

Here are some of the exercises recommended by Betty Edwards, and other teachers, for enhancing creativity by switching into R-mode.

Exercise 1

1 Find a line drawing in a book or magazine. You're going to be copying it, so it needs to be of a reasonable size. Once you've selected something, don't look at it again until you start to draw.

2 Find a fairly soft pencil (say a 3B or 4B), a pencil sharpener, a rubber and some clean sheets of paper.

3 Turn the book so the image is upside down. Now copy the line drawing giving no thought at all to what it represents but only thinking of it as a kind of puzzle in which you have to get the lines and spaces the right size and in the correct relationship to one another. Spend at least half an hour making your copy, more

if it's large or complicated. Don't turn either your own drawing or the original around until you're done.

Insight

Your finished drawing should astonish you. How can you be so much better as an artist of the upside down than as an artist of the 'normal' world? The answer is that you're far less likely to introduce your preconceived ideas about what the thing *should* look like. Instead, you're working entirely in terms of abstract patterns, causing you to engage your right brain.

Exercise 2

1 Tape a wad of three or four sheets of paper onto a drawing board or tabletop – the idea is to create a comfortable drawing surface that can't move.

2 Set an alarm to go off in five minutes.

3 Sit at your makeshift 'easel', pencil in hand poised to start drawing, but face right away from it so you can't actually see what you're doing.

4 Look, instead, at your other non-drawing hand, which is what you're going to be using as a model. You'll need to rest the back of that hand on something like a shelf or the back of a chair so you can comfortably keep it still.

5 Crinkle the palm of your non-drawing hand a little so you create plenty of creases. It's those that you're going to be copying.

6 Place your pencil in the middle of the paper, gaze at a crease and draw it. At no time can you look at what you're drawing. Imagine, instead, that there's some kind of mechanical link between your eyes and your drawing hand. As your eyes track along a crease, bit by bit, so your drawing hand moves.

7 When you've finished one crease move on to another and another until the five-minute alarm rings. Of course, what you're drawing is unlikely to be very much like the actual creases in your palm but that doesn't matter. Resist the temptation to check-up on how the drawing is going. Only turn to look when the allotted time is up.

Insight

This time you may not find your drawing is very accurate. It's almost impossible that it will be. But you will have forced your brain to switch into R-mode. At the same time, you will have made some quite beautiful marks – and come to appreciate the palm of your hand in a way you never did before.

And if you're not very creative?

How would you feel if, as you were about to board a flight, you overheard the captain saying, 'You know, I think I'll try flying this thing upside down for a change'? Or suppose you were about to be wheeled into the operating theatre when you heard the surgeon say, 'Guess what, I'm fed up doing this operation the usual way – I think I'll try something different this time.'

In reality, there are numerous situations in which creativity is *not* called for. In fact, in which creativity would be a definite negative. Most situations, in all probability. Just sit back and think for a moment about a world in which everyone is always striving to come up with original ways of doing things. It would certainly be stimulating but it would also be highly chaotic and dangerous.

So I've now done my best to make you feel relaxed about 'not being creative'. But I hope I've also demonstrated the advantages of being able to see things in new ways and to come up with new ideas. We can probably all do with more of that. Here are some ways you can increase your creativity:

- ▶ Regularly practise divergent thinking exercises like those above.
- ▶ Give your right-brain a workout and improve your hand/eye co-ordination by sketching.
- ▶ When you look at illustrations of any kind, try to work out what the people are thinking; make up stories about what they were doing before and what they'll do afterwards.

- ▶ Whenever a politician announces a new policy, try to foresee as many problems with it as you can.
- ▶ Whenever you hear of a problem, try to think of as many possible solutions as you can.
- ▶ Be curious – when you're curious you start to see the things other people don't see and you start looking in new ways and from new angles.

Answers to the linking words test
1 Nail (nail polish, nail file, nailbrush)
2 Crack (crack of the whip, crack of dawn, crack shot)
3 Double (double time, double back, double act)
4 Canada (They're all in it)
5 Cat (Catalan, cat-o'-nine-tails, catgut)

10 TIPS FOR SUCCESS

1 Creativity is valuable in many things other than art.

2 Psychologists associate creativity with high Openness but it may require above average Neuroticism to drive it.

3 Convergent thinking is the ability to deduce a single solution to a problem by following rules.

4 Divergent thinking is the ability to generate multiple solutions to a problem by breaking rules or 'thinking outside the box'.

5 Creative people are good at divergent thinking.

6 Ellis Paul Torrance saw fluency (numbers of ideas), originality, and detail as the key elements in creative thinking.

7 Roger Sperry has argued that each hemisphere of the brain is a conscious system in its own right.

8 The left side of your brain, good with words and numbers, is your 'bank manager personality'; the right side, good with images, is your 'hippie personality'.

9 You can force the right side of your brain to take over by practising vision-based exercises.

10 No matter how lacking in creativity you may consider yourself to be, you can improve by following various exercises.

8

How nice are you?

In this chapter you will learn:
- *why you may not be as nice as you think*
- *how obedience to authority and conformism can make people do bad things*
- *why altruism may be in your most selfish best interests.*

Before we get going, let's just find out a little bit more about you.
Tick any of the following with which you agree and write down your score:

1 My country right or wrong.
2 My country is the best country in the world.
3 My religion is the true religion and all other religions are wrong.
4 I would have far more in common with any of my countrymen than someone from another country.
5 I would feel very uncomfortable if I dressed in a way very different from other people.
6 Team games are important for teaching team spirit.
7 It's essential to do what the team captain says.
8 School uniforms are good because they create a sense of belonging.
9 Human beings need a leader, otherwise there would just be anarchy.
10 If large numbers of people believe something, that proves there must be something in it.

So how did you get on? If you ticked all or most items you probably won't be surprised to learn that you're very conformist and quite likely low in Openness. And you're no doubt quite happy with that. There are no rights and wrongs in terms of personality traits, as I've said before. They simply convey different advantages and disadvantages. If you ticked none or very few, then you're very individualistic and probably high in Openness. And, again, you're probably pretty happy with that.

Now let's try to find out how nice you are. For a change I'm not going to give you any cunning tests designed to trip you up. I'm just going to ask you for your own opinion. Here we go: How nice are you?

Pretty nice, eh? You do your best to get on with other people, you help them when you can, you give money to charity. Yes, that's nice. But, you see, almost everyone is nice when there's no serious problem. The fact that you're almost always nice may simply mean that you almost always don't face any serious problems.

To know how nice you really are we need to know how you react in various different, more trying circumstances.

The Milgram experiment

Suppose you were asked to help further the cause of science by assisting in an experiment. The purpose of the experiment, conducted by a scientist, is to study the effect of punishment on learning. Your task is to operate a console that is capable of giving electric shocks to another volunteer. This other volunteer, strapped into a special chair inside a booth, will be asked questions. When there's a wrong answer you're to flick a switch labelled '15 volts – Slight Shock'. If the volunteer keeps giving wrong answers, the level of the shocks will be increased. The final switch is labelled '450 volts – Danger: Severe Shock'.

What would you, a 'nice' person according to your own assessment, actually do? Perhaps you would refuse to take part on the grounds that it all sounds a little unpleasant. But, then, the volunteer in the chair isn't objecting and, after all, this is a scientific experiment. Perhaps you would assist the cause of science only until the volunteer in the chair showed signs of serious discomfort. Certainly you would never flick the switch labelled 'Moderate Shock' let alone touch the final switch. Would you?

This was exactly the scenario set up by the social psychologist Stanley Milgram in 1961. In fact, the volunteer in the chair was a stooge and no electric current actually passed. But the succession of men (and in a subsequent experiment, women) who operated the console didn't know that. When the stooge screamed and groaned they thought it was for real, when he begged to be released they thought it was for real, and when he slumped in the chair as if unconscious or dead, they thought it was for real.

To encourage the volunteers, Milgram used such standard phrases as, 'The experiment requires that you continue' or 'You have no other choice, you must go on.' In that first experiment involving 40 'nice' volunteers, all went beyond 'Moderate Shock' and 25 went all the way to delivering the maximum voltage. On the plus side, 15 people did refuse to deliver the maximum shock. On the minus side, none of the 15 demanded that the experiment itself be terminated nor went to check the health of the stooge.

Of course, as soon as the significance of Milgram's experiment was made public, politicians and teachers, not only in the USA but all over the world, rushed to change the teaching system. Out went things such as school uniforms, team games, a belief in the superiority of particular nationalities or ethnic groups and, most important of all, obedience to authority.

Well, no, it wasn't quite like that. Actually, nothing changed. And since then we've had, among others, the My Lai Massacre in South Vietnam, the Rwandan Genocide, and the Srebrenica Genocide. Even so, we have evolved, haven't we? 'Nice' people wouldn't behave the same way today as in that original experiment, would they?

I'm afraid they would. Dr Thomas Blass reviewed all the Milgram-like experiments in the 25 years up to 1985 and found no suggestion of any improvement. And in the first decade of the twenty-first century, his experiment has been replicated, in more or less the same way, several times (by, for example, Jerry M. Burger in 2006, by the BBC's *Horizon* programme in 2009, and for a French documentary *Le Jeu de la Mort* which used a game show variation). Always the results have been about the same – around two-thirds of people give the highest shock. In fact, in *Le Jeu de la Mort* (The Game of Death) the level was 80 per cent.

Why do so many of us act like this? One explanation is the 'agentic state theory'. In other words, once you see yourself as merely an agent acting on the instructions of an authority you no longer see yourself as responsible.

As Milgram wrote: 'Each individual possesses a conscience… But when he merges his person into an organizational structure, a new creature replaces autonomous man…mindful only of the sanctions of authority.'

Now, you did write down your score for the questionnaire at the beginning of the chapter, didn't you? Hold onto that number. Because, another theory is that the more conformist you are, the more likely you are to do what an authority figure asks. Support for this view comes from the fact that levels of obedience were found to be slightly higher in the more authoritarian areas of East Asia and in Muslim cultures, while levels were significantly lower in Brazil, Costa Rica, Nigeria, and the Ivory Coast, and among the Inuit of Canada.

Insight

Milgram went on to explore several variations on his experiment. He found that when the stooge was a woman rather than a man, there was no significant effect on the outcome. Nor was there when the volunteer at the console was a woman – it's thought that women's greater empathy was negated by their tendency to be more in awe of authority. But, interestingly, that authority diminished for both men and women when the scientist gave instructions by telephone, rather than being in the room.

Self-coaching tip

Is there anything you could do as a potential victim to influence your tormentor? Milgram found that when the stooge was brought closer to the volunteer at the console, the degree of compliance decreased. In other words, the more you can help yourself to be viewed as a human being with feelings, the more empathy you can evoke.

Conformism

So let's examine this business of conformism a little more closely.

American psychologist Solomon Asch asked volunteers to take part in an experiment with eight other people who, unknown to the volunteers, were stooges. All were asked to say which of three lines on a card was the same length as a single line on a second card. Three-quarters of the volunteers were swayed by the plainly incorrect answer called out by the other eight 'volunteers' (who, of course, had been directed by Asch to give the wrong answer). Even the quarter who insisted on the correct line were very nervous about their judgements.

Why would people go against the evidence of their own senses? Well, that's conformity for you. And what makes this particular experiment all the more dramatic is that people were conforming with others they'd never met before and about whose judgement they had no knowledge. When people voluntarily form a group, things become even more interesting.

What would be your gut feeling?

▶ When people form a committee, decisions would be most likely to follow a safe, middle course.
▶ When people form a committee, decisions would be most likely to follow an extreme course.

If you plumped for the first option, then your gut feeling, along with most people's, would be wrong. Committee decisions tend to be *more* extreme than the opinions of the individuals making up the committee.

In one experiment, committee members were asked what degree of risk they would accept when making an investment. Later, they were asked to take that very decision as a committee and, counter intuitively, they opted for greater risk.

Why is there this so-called 'risky shift'? Here are the reasons:

▶ Once the group attitude is clear, you'll gain the approval of the group by being the same, only more so.
▶ To be one of the leaders implies being ahead of, and therefore more extreme than, the others (who then catch-up).
▶ Group responsibility reduces the fear of failure.

GROUP MEETS GROUP, GROUP FIGHTS GROUP

So groups tend to be more extreme than individuals. What happens, then, when one group comes up against another? Social psychologist

Muzafer Sherif decided to find out, using white, middle-class Protestant boys at his own, special summer camp as his subjects.

For the first three days or so the boys were left to form their own individual friendships. Only when that had happened were they split into two groups. As far as possible, the friends were separated. Did the pals stay pals? Not at all. The original friendships petered out as the two groups formed their own identities, giving themselves 'gang' names and adopting their own slang.

The next stage of the experiment was for Sherif to introduce competitive games. Initially, the boys played in a friendly enough way but as the days went by, so the boys increasingly broke the rules of the games and became violent. Each group blamed the other for starting the trouble. Eventually one group attacked the other group at night and it all ended with the two groups being unable to share the same dining room.

Insight

Why is there this tendency towards group identity? One reason is that, in order to benefit from the obvious protection of a group, our ancestors had to show that they were 'in'. Another is that humans have succeeded by being good imitators, learning from other people by observing them and copying them. Unfortunately, the trait can be carried to dangerous extremes. As the philosopher Eric Hoffer wrote, 'When people are free to do as they please, they usually imitate each other.' The Sherif experiment certainly proved that, contrary to what is often said, competitive sport does nothing to improve relationships between countries.

Self-coaching tip

Although conformism has many negatives, it has to be said that it can also be used in a positive way. Organizations such as Alcoholics Anonymous exploit it by getting members to make a public commitment in front of fellow sufferers. That vow then becomes more difficult to break. Similar tactics can be used to motivate any group of people – a sales team, for example.

The Stanford prison experiment

By now you're probably looking for evidence that the human race isn't as black as I'm trying to make out. After all, you may be saying, the people in the Milgram experiment weren't inflicting pain because they wanted to. They were taking part in what they thought was a useful experiment under the direction of a man who said he was a scientist. And that's what made the Stanford prison experiment even more unsettling.

On a Sunday morning in 1971 in Palo Alto, California, 24 student volunteers flipped coins. As a result, half became 'prisoners' and half became 'guards' in a mock prison in the basement of Stanford University. Psychology professor Philip Zimbardo's experiment had begun. It was planned to run for two weeks. In the event, the situation in the 'prison' turned so nasty so quickly that it had to be ended after just six days.

The 'prisoners' were made to strip naked to be deloused with a spray, had to put on stocking caps to approximate having their heads shaven, were given a numbered smock to wear, and were fitted with a permanent ankle chain. The idea, given the brevity of the experiment, was to accelerate development of a 'prisoner mentality'.

As to the guards – and this is important – they were given no specific training. They were free, within limits, to act as they thought guards should in order to maintain discipline. They could be nice or they could be nasty. They were provided with khaki uniforms, billy clubs borrowed from the police, and mirrored sunglasses.

It was on the second morning that the 'prisoners' made their move. They ripped off their caps and numbers and barricaded themselves inside their cells. After holding a meeting, the 'guards' decided to respond with force. They used the icy stream from fire extinguishers to force the 'prisoners' back, stripped them naked, removed their beds and put the ringleaders into solitary confinement. They also decided to use psychological tactics. One of the three cells became a 'privilege cell' in which 'good prisoners' could have beds, washing facilities and better food. The effect was to break the solidarity among the prisoners. But it became even more cunning than that. Half a day later some 'good prisoners' were sent back to the ordinary cells and some 'bad prisoners' were put into the 'privilege cell'. Now none of the prisoners knew who could be trusted and who might be informers. As a further refinement, 'prisoners' were made to defecate in a bucket which, if they didn't co-operate, might be left in the cell.

The first 'prisoner', 8612, had a breakdown after just 36 hours and – once Professor Zimbardo was convinced he was genuine – was released. This was a key moment because, soon after, a 'guard' overheard 'prisoners' talking about an escape plan, which 8612 was supposedly organizing from the outside. To foil it, the 'prisoners' were moved to a new location and chained together with bags over their heads. When no plot developed, the guards were unnerved and reacted in frustration with even more physical aggression and even more psychological cunning.

What's fascinating in the Stanford prisoner experiment is the way everyone played their roles to perfection, as if they were actors. But they weren't acting. First of all there were the prisoners. Any of them, if they'd insisted, could have left at any time. After all, they were volunteers. They even went before a mock parole board, pleaded to be released, then returned meekly to their cells. It was as if a switch had been moved inside their heads. They had started out by playing a role and had become so confused they now seemed to believe it was all real. What made it all the more shocking was that it had happened in such a short time.

As to the 'parole board', it was headed by a man who genuinely had been a prisoner in San Quentin. Did he now 'do unto others' as he wished others had done to him? On the contrary. He was later said to have been astonished and sickened at his own behaviour.

The 'guards' fell into three stereotypes. There were the 'good guys' who did favours for the prisoners and never punished them. There were the 'tough but fair' who followed the rules. And there were the 'hostiles' who enjoyed the power they wielded. But no one ever came late for work, or ducked out of a shift, and not even the 'good guys' asked for the experiment to be ended.

> **Insight**
> Worryingly, the psychologists hadn't been able to predict which guard would be which type from the pre-experiment personality tests. Although there were plenty of moderate individuals, the policy of the guards as a group became one of physical and psychological abuse – an example of the 'risky-shift' at work in a group of men.

Head of the 'prison' was Professor Zimbardo himself, in the role of Prison Superintendent. He, too, 'forgot' that he was conducting an experiment and began acting like a real superintendent, more concerned that there should be no problem in 'his jail' than for the welfare of his volunteers.

There had even been a visiting day, just like a real prison, to which parents had come, and a genuine priest. In all, about 50 outsiders had visited the 'prison' and none had raised any objections. Not until, that is, the 'fairy princess'.

Surely a 'fairy princess' should have been in some other scenario? She certainly hadn't been anticipated. But on the fifth night this stereotype, too, appeared in the person of graduate student Christina Maslach, interested to see what was going on. It was her appalled reaction that made Zimbardo wake up to the realization that things had gone too far.

Next morning Zimbardo ended the experiment, only half way through. It had become too 'powerful'. The 'prisoners' were described as 'disintegrated' both as a group and as individuals. They were just 'hanging on' and reacting in pathological ways. The 'guards' had complete control. All in less than six days.

The experiment had at least one happy ending. Zimbardo and Maslach were later married.

The Hofling experiment

It's easy to see the relevance of the Milgram and Stanford experiments in situations such as warfare. But in everyday life is a bit of conformism really a problem? If people overreact to authority, is it such a big deal? Then consider the Hofling experiment.

Psychiatrist Charles K. Hofling arranged for nurses at a hospital in the USA to be called by a fictitious 'Dr Smith' and asked to administer 20 mg of a fictional drug 'Astroten' to a patient. 'Dr Smith' said he would deal with the paperwork later. The 'Astroten' had previously been placed in the drugs cabinet by the experimenter and the label stated that 10 mg was the safe dose.

Of 22 nurses telephoned, 21 went to administer the unsafe dose, but were stopped. What's particularly interesting is that this experiment created a conflict between *two* authorities. On the one hand, the nurses were trained to follow certain procedures (such as requiring paperwork beforehand, and only giving drugs on the drugs list). But at the same time they were also trained to obey the orders of doctors. In this case the fictional doctor 'won', even though he was unknown to the nurses and giving instructions by telephone (which the Milgram experiment showed to be less effective than giving instructions in person).

The implications for murdering someone simply by making a telephone call are obvious. But it's worse than that. Patients have had the wrong organs removed, and at least one plane has crashed, after junior staff failed to point out what they knew was an error. Why? Fear of authority.

I'm nice, I give to charity

Have you given any money to charity this year? Probably, yes. Most of us have one way or another. Perhaps you've 'adopted' a child or an animal, put some coins into a collection box, joined a society dedicated to making the world a better place in some way, or deliberately bought a product on the grounds that a percentage of the price would be used for a good cause.

What about your time? Most of us would rather give money than hours. So it's rather less likely that you've volunteered to help in an old people's home, sold second-hand clothes in a charity shop or cleaned a pond to make it fit for frogs and newts.

Fewer still would have given blood, acted as guinea pigs for new drugs or – rarest of all – chosen to put their lives on the line in battle.

But if you have done any of these things, why? What's in it for you? If Darwin's theory of natural selection is right, such altruistic acts, apparently against your own best interests, surely shouldn't occur. Don't they prove that, in fact, you really, really are nice after all?

Well, actually, no. Do you remember that conundrum posed in Chapter 1? The one called The Prisoner's Dilemma? Do you remember how tit for tat turned out to be the best policy? Well, it turns out that your altruism, everyone's altruism, is nothing more than a strategy of tit for tat in a real-life version of the game.

This has been pretty convincingly argued by the biologist Richard Dawkins. He rests his case on his theory of the 'selfish gene' and on the work of political scientist Robert Axelrod and evolutionary biologist W. D. Hamilton. Dawkins argues that anything that lives – you, a dog, an ant, a tree – is just a 'machine' to ensure the survival of genes. So humans are not really the top things on planet Earth. Genes are. When a 'survival machine' is successful and increases in numbers, so the genes are successful and proliferate. When a 'survival machine' is unsuccessful and declines, so the genes head for extinction.

The essential features of The Prisoner's Dilemma, you may recall, were that you and another player each have two cards, one labelled 'Co-operate' and the other 'Defect', thus giving four possible outcomes. The cards are not turned over until both of you have played. For each outcome a banker would pay out as follows:

▶ You both played 'Co-operate'. You each win 300 units (pounds, dollars, ounces of gold or whatever).
▶ You both played 'Defect'. You are each fined 10 units.
▶ You played 'Co-operate', the other person played 'Defect'. You are fined 100 units; the other person wins 500 units.
▶ You played 'Defect', the other person played 'Co-operate'. You win 500 units; the other person is fined 100 units.

For a single game, if your opponent has played 'Defect', the best you can do is also play 'Defect', which incurs a fine of 10 units (if you played 'Co-operate' the fine would be 100 units). But if your opponent has played 'Co-operate' the best you can do is still to play 'Defect', which wins 500 units (as opposed to 300 units if you also played Co-operate). Your strategy therefore must be to play your 'Defect' card and, by the same reasoning, the other player must do the same. So you both play 'Defect', you're both 'nasty' rather than 'nice', and it doesn't get you very far.

Of course, we're not actually interested in the game itself. We're trying to find out what particular life strategy would have an evolutionary advantage. And in real life, unless losing one game is fatal, you get the opportunity to play many, many games, evaluating people both as individuals and in general as you do so. To approximate real life, the game of The Prisoner's Dilemma therefore needs to be played over and over.

When that happens, something interesting occurs.

Axelrod ran a competition, inviting experts in games theory to submit winning strategies for The Prisoner's Dilemma. What kinds of strategies could there be? Well, you could have 'Always Defect' or 'Always Co-operate' or 'Co-operate most of the time but play Defect at random now and then' and so on. He received 14 strategies and brought some very powerful computers to bear on the matter. After 200 moves, the tit for tat strategy was declared the winner.

Tit for Tat is a 'nice' strategy. You play 'Co-operate' on the first hand and on subsequent hands you simply copy whatever the other player did on the previous hand. If the other player is also nice and plays 'Co-operate' so you follow with 'Co-operate' too. If he or she plays 'Defect', you punish that behaviour by playing 'Defect' in the next round.

Nobody submitted a strategy that might have been encapsulated by the name 'tit for two tats'. That's to say, there would be no retaliation until two defections. But Axelrod worked out that if they had, they would have won.

So, to the surprise of many, niceness and forgiveness turned out to be winning qualities.

A second round attracted 62 entries and, again, niceness and forgiveness came out on top.

How does all this relate to real life? It doesn't take a lot of imagination. I ask you for a favour and you agree. The following week you ask me for a favour in return. I refuse. It looks like my selfish behaviour has made me the winner. I got something for nothing. But let's continue the game of life. Another week later, I again need a favour. This time you refuse, because I let you down before. Not only that, but you've told everyone else I can't be trusted. Nobody will do me the favour. I'm on my own.

Putting it crudely, anyone whose genes predispose them to cheating in the game of favours may gain a short-term advantage but will be doomed in the long run. By contrast, anyone whose genes predispose them to being co-operative may suffer a short-term cost but will benefit in the long run.

Insight

It could be argued that tit for tat works within a small community – birds removing one another's ticks, or cleaner-fish removing parasites from larger fish – but will break down in a world inhabited by billions of mobile people. In such a world you can cheat and move on. But, in fact, we're living in an ever smaller world, making it ever harder to get away with cheating. Stanley Milgram, whom we've already met, asked various people chosen at random in Omaha and Wichita to forward packages to a person in Boston. If, by chance, they happened to know the contact on first name terms (extremely unlikely), they could forward the package directly. Otherwise they were to send it on to someone else they did know on first name terms who might have a better chance of knowing the contact. In 232 out of 296 cases, the chain was broken by someone refusing to take part. But of the 64 packages that did arrive, the average path length was just under six people. Although Milgram himself never used the phrase, others have dubbed this 'six degrees of separation'. Recently, similar experiments have been conducted on the internet with more or less the same result.

Self-coaching tip

A great deal of emphasis is placed on competition in business but you should never forget the power of co-operation, either, whether in business or in your personal life.

What does it really prove?

So how nice are you really? What have we learned?

Stanley Milgram has demonstrated that most people are capable of terrible things when acting under authority. Professor Philip Zimbardo has demonstrated that some people are capable of terrible things when put in positions of authority. Muzafer Sherif has demonstrated that even arbitrary membership of a group makes people hostile to non-members. And Richard Dawkins has demonstrated that even when you're being nice, you're not at all – it's simply a strategy for gene survival.

It's a pretty bleak picture, isn't it?

Have the experiments themselves done any good? Certainly one of the volunteers in the original 1961 experiment later wrote to Milgram saying that he was refusing the draft for the Vietnam war and was 'fully prepared to go to jail' if necessary. But there's no evidence that society in general has learned much.

Of his experiment, Professor Zimbardo concluded: 'We realized how ordinary people could be readily transformed from the good Dr. Jekyll to the evil Mr. Hyde.'

Stanley Milgram's comment was perhaps even more frightening: 'Often it is not so much the kind of person a man is as the kind of situation in which he finds himself that determines how he will act.'

Self-coaching tip

This lesson is so important I'm sorry to be offering it as a mere tip. It's a lesson for every individual and for a better world and it's very clear. No matter how nice, moral and strong-willed you consider yourself to be, never willingly put yourself into a position in which you might be called upon to act in a way you'd regret.

10 TIPS FOR SUCCESS

1 Most people act nicely when they're not under pressure – it's how they behave in difficult circumstances that really counts.

2 Around two-thirds of people are willing to inflict pain on others when instructed to do so by an authority figure.

3 In one experiment, three-quarters of participants conformed with the majority view, even though it was plainly wrong.

4 Committee decisions tend to be *more* extreme than the opinions of the individuals making up the committee.

5 Even when arbitrarily assigned to groups, people still take on the group identity.

6 When people are put into positions of authority, a significant proportion are likely to abuse their power.

7 Human beings (and all living things) can be considered simply as 'machines' to ensure the survival of genes.

8 Usually it benefits genes when their 'machines' act 'selfishly' but sometimes altruism pays.

9 Life can be seen as a game of The Prisoner's Dilemma in which the best strategy is tit for tat.

10 It may be that we all act according to the role assigned to us in any given situation.

9

Successfully happy

In this chapter you will learn:
- *the difference between internal and external happiness*
- *how to increase your internal happiness*
- *how to increase your external happiness.*

In the Big Five system there's no specific trait of happiness. Some
people might think that's curious. But happiness is seen as a transient
emotion rather than a permanent characteristic. In terms of Big
Five traits, you'll probably find it easier to be happy if you're low
in Neuroticism and Conscientiousness, and high in Extroversion,
Agreeableness and Openness. However, I would argue that a higher
or lower state of happiness can be sufficiently permanent to be
considered a personality trait. In this chapter I'll certainly be aiming
for you to enjoy a consistently higher state of happiness than you do
now.

Before we can start to increase it, we have to find out where
happiness comes from. Can you, for example, make yourself happy
by doing all kinds of nice things? By, say, spending money on clothes
or holidays? Or is it more to do with ironing out the kinks in your
personality and developing better control of your mind?

In other words, is happiness external or internal?

Here's how the 'internals' argue. There are many things that happen
in life that are beyond your control. If you base your happiness on
externals, you'll forever be on a rollercoaster, alternating between
exhilaration when things are good and despair when things go badly.
However, when you have the ability to generate a state of happiness
internally, so you're no longer dependent on forces beyond your
control, you can always be happy.

And here's how the 'externals' argue. To be happy when life is bad is not only difficult, it's also a form of insanity. The best way to stop yourself feeling hungry is to eat and, in the same way, the best way to stop yourself feeling unhappy is to 'consume' things to cheer yourself up. You can't just be happy for no reason, so give yourself a reason.

And here's my 'arbitration'. Why choose? The two things are not mutually exclusive. You can work on both your internal and external happiness at the same time. And you should.

Self-coaching tip

The first step towards being happy is simply to *make a conscious decision to be happier*. Don't imagine that happiness is something that falls down on you like rain. Happiness is very much under your personal control. Unless you're seriously depressed, you always have the option of choosing how to look at things, whether to focus on the good or the bad, on the bright side or the dark.

Internal happiness

One day, when you were an infant, a witch presented you with four possible paths and asked you to choose. The path that you selected would forevermore determine your relationship with the world and, to a considerable extent, your future happiness.

These were the paths:

▶ **Path 1** – I'm all right and you're all right.
▶ **Path 2** – I'm all right but you're not all right.
▶ **Path 3** – I'm not all right but you're all right.
▶ **Path 4** – I'm not all right and you're not all right.

And you chose...

Well, that's my little fairy story but, in essence, it's almost certainly correct. Most psychologists believe that infants fairly quickly develop one of the four attitudes and cling to it throughout their lives.

You've probably grasped that the path most conducive to happiness is the first. You accept yourself as you are and you accept others the same way. That doesn't mean you think you're perfect. Rather, you know that neither you nor anyone else *can* be perfect. But that's okay. You don't beat yourself up over it. In the words of the song, you're one of those people who needs people, and you're one of the luckiest (and happiest) people in the world.

If you opted for the second path, you almost certainly make exceptions for a few 'chosen' ones. Your partner...your parents... your children. Nevertheless, you're liable to develop hostile feelings even towards them if you think you've been criticized or betrayed in any way. As for everyone else on the planet, they're to be treated as enemies unless and until they've proven otherwise. You see every person as a potential threat and you're always on your guard. You can be happy, but only when you've hidden yourself and those close to you away from the world.

The third path is very different. Everyone else seems to be better off than you in every way. They're more accomplished, more successful, more attractive, more deserving and, of course, happier. But, worthless though you are, you can at least see that something better exists. There is some hope. For those on the fourth path, no such hope exists. Everything is black. If you're on that path, you're frequently depressed.

In reality, you don't so much choose a path as have it chosen for you. You'll already be *inclined* towards one of the four on the basis of your genes. And if your early experiences seem to confirm its essential truth, then that's the one you'll follow.

Self-coaching tip

Now that you know Path 1 (I'm all right and you're all right) is the path that leads to happiness, all you have to do is adopt that manner of thinking. Simple! Well, of course, it's not *quite* that simple. But you *can* learn to change the way you think. You *can* learn to reduce the number and intensity of negative thoughts about yourself and other people, and to increase the number and intensity of your positive thoughts. One system for doing exactly that is known as cognitive therapy (CT) and we'll be taking a look at it in Chapter 12. For the moment, just try making lists of all the good things about yourself, and about most of the people you come into contact with. Although, as we saw in the previous chapter, most people can be subverted into doing bad things, you'll hopefully see that the way of the world is far more Path 1 than anything else.

Dealing with anger

Can you be happy when you're angry? That would seem to be pretty difficult. So here's a little test to see how angry you are. Not just how angry you get from time to time, but to root out if there's an undercurrent of anger that's always present.

On a scale of 1 to 10, rate how accurately the following statements describe you or represent your thoughts (1 meaning 'not at all accurate' and 10 meaning 'entirely accurate').

What makes you angry?
- ☐ I get extremely angry when something or somebody gets in my way.
- ☐ I get extremely angry when I can't do something as well as I think I should.
- ☐ I get extremely angry when the world is unfair to me or to others I care about.
- ☐ I get extremely angry when I'm held back by the incompetence of other people.
- ☐ I get extremely angry when I don't get the recognition or success that I deserve.

How easily do you get angry?
- ☐ Those close to me say I get extremely angry more often than most people.
- ☐ I get extremely angry at least once a day.
- ☐ Often I feel angry without knowing why.
- ☐ I can make myself extremely angry by thinking of unjust things that have happened to me in the past.
- ☐ Once I'm angry it takes me an extremely long time to calm down.

How hostile are you?
- ☐ It infuriates me when deference is shown to so-called experts who plainly don't know any more than I do.

- [ ] I don't trust someone till they've shown they can be trusted.
- [ ] I don't like people unless they give me a reason to like them.
- [ ] It's important to remember that human beings are the most dangerous animals on the planet.
- [ ] There should be a lot more people in prison.

How do you express your anger?
- [ ] I harbour grudges for a long time.
- [ ] I may have to wait but I make sure I get even in the end.
- [ ] I remember all the occasions on which I've been treated badly.
- [ ] Even if I explain what's wrong, that doesn't make the anger go away.
- [ ] I can't show how I feel because that would be just too dangerous.

How did you score? There were five questions in each of four categories, making a maximum possible score of 200 (and a minimum of 20).

If your total score was:

▶ **150–200:** you're clearly a very angry person and that's the subtext to your day and your life. You're seldom happy unless something *makes* you happy. On the other hand, without some happy event you remain irritable and, for that reason, quite a lot of people avoid you. Professional help in dealing with your anger might be a good idea.

▶ **100–149:** you're certainly not the kind of person others go in fear of, but you are spoiling your own life by the unbalanced views you hold and the way you deal with your emotions. Spend some time reflecting on your attitude and, using the ideas in this chapter, work on building a more positive outlook.

▶ **60–99:** you get angry when there's a good reason to feel angry but otherwise you're not an angry or irritable person. You empathize with others and realize that no one, including yourself, can be perfect. Members of your family and friends have their faults but, set against the pleasure you derive from their company, they're too trivial to mention.

▶ **20–59:** you're a saint. You have a smile on your face everywhere you go. Very little makes you angry. You don't take very many problems personally and you deal with difficulties calmly.

> ### Self-coaching tip
>
> You get good at what you practise. That's why anger is something that tends to build on itself. The more you get angry, the more you mould your brain into an 'angry brain' by strengthening what might be called the 'anger synapses'. That's why the popular advice to let your anger explode is completely wrong. Think of a saucepan that's boiling over. Yes, it may help a bit to take the lid off, but the problem will only really be solved by turning the heat down. Discuss what's upset you, yes. That's important. But once you let your pulse get over 100, you'll lose your ability to discuss things rationally. In the jargon, you'll be 'flooded' with chemicals more suited to fighting than conciliating. So no shouting, no yelling, no punching pillows. Calm down and then deal with the situation.

How to stop worrying

As we've seen, people who worry a lot have a negative emotion system that's more responsive than the average. In other words, they're high in the Big Five trait of Neuroticism (see Chapter 1). It's not easy to change a personality trait (although we'll be having a good go later in the book) but it is nevertheless possible to reduce the amount you worry.

Have a look at the following statements and tick the ones that apply to you.

- ☐ I think worrying is a sign that I'm a sincere and concerned sort of person.
- ☐ By worrying, I have a better chance of finding a solution.
- ☐ I can't relax if I don't know how things are being organized over the next hours and days.
- ☐ Worrying often makes it difficult for me to sleep at night.
- ☐ Even when I think I have a solution, uncertainty makes it difficult for me to act.
- ☐ I wouldn't want to be a person who didn't worry because that would mean I was callous.

- ☐ My life has been a whole series of calamities.
- ☐ It's important to be vigilant for hidden dangers at all times.

If you ticked all or most of the boxes, then you're not just a person who worries a lot, you're someone who worries unnecessarily. Generally speaking, most of the things we worry about never actually happen. And those that do happen often just aren't as bad as we thought they would be. So that's a lot of pointless worrying. Let's try to find out exactly how much. Buy a little notebook and each time you notice yourself worrying about something, write it down. As time goes by, note whether or not the thing you were worrying about actually happened. If it did happen, give it a score from 10 for 'truly awful' down to 1 for 'hardly bothered me at all'. After a suitable period, analyse your findings. I think you'll be surprised. I predict that very few of the things you feared actually did happen and those that did weren't as bad as you imagined.

Another way of tackling the worrying problem is to play the 'So what?' game. Let's say you're afraid of failing an exam. Then ask yourself: 'So what would be the consequences?' Maybe you can take the exam again later. Maybe failing would be a good thing, signalling that you're targeting the wrong subject and should switch to something else where you'll be happier. Maybe you'll switch teachers and discover a mentor who will become an important influence on your life. Certainly nothing terrible will happen. After playing 'So what?' you'll probably conclude that failing an exam (or whatever) isn't quite so serious after all.

Insight

A problem with worrying is that it seldom leads to action. Worriers tend to become demoralized and even depressed. They can't seem to raise the energy to tackle things. As a result, problems pile up, giving even more cause for worry. It all becomes a circular trap, building on itself. Not every problem has a solution but most of them do. And even those that don't have ways in which the consequences can be reduced. So don't hide from problems; tackle them as far as you can. Get help when necessary – and, of course, a chat with a friend can at least make you feel a bit better.

Self-coaching tip

Make it a rule to tackle problems promptly during the day. As bedtime approaches, tell yourself you've done as much as anybody can do. Remind yourself it's your *duty* to get a good night's sleep so you can be fresh and ready to tackle things again the following day. Recall that worrying will only reduce your effectiveness and therefore be a betrayal of yourself and those you're trying to help.

Insight

A useful technique for letting go of both anger and your worries is dissociation. When you're really annoyed or worried about something then, in your mind, you probably see it 'close up'. You make it as vivid as possible and, consequently, make your emotions equally strong. In order to let go, you need to do the opposite. You need to dissociate as far as possible by pulling back the 'camera' of your mind's eye, just as a camera pulls back in a film. As a result, your negative emotions will be much weaker and more easily dealt with. It's a particularly useful technique for handling unhappy situations about which, in practical terms, you can do absolutely nothing.

Meditation

How could it be possible that sitting cross-legged and thinking about nothing very much at all could have even a remote impact on happiness? Put like that it doesn't sound very likely. Yet the evidence is there. People who meditate regularly say they feel happier; scientists can measure the increase in 'happy chemicals'; and several physical indicators of wellbeing also improve. Researchers have monitored the brains of people who begin meditating and found that, over a period of months, activity tends to increase in the frontal lobe of the left-brain. That's the part associated with higher moods and optimism.

You might access your inner happiness in your very first session but it takes most people a few weeks. Thereafter, meditation deepens until, perhaps after a year or two, something very profound is experienced. Almost everyone talks of feeling calmer and more peaceful. Accompanying these feelings are those of patience and compassion. Later come feelings of intense joy. And all this, in turn, leads to a more positive engagement with life.

HOW TO MEDITATE

You can meditate at any time, in many different sorts of places and in a variety of positions. The important things are to choose a time you can stick to (every day or every few days), a quiet place in which you won't be disturbed, and a posture you can maintain.

The pose traditionally associated with meditation is the lotus position – but I certainly wouldn't recommend it to begin with. It involves sitting on the floor with the right foot on the left thigh and the left foot on the right thigh, so that the left ankle crosses over on top of the right ankle. The idea behind it is that it's extremely stable so that, in deep meditation, you won't topple over. At the same time, it's not a position in which it's easy to fall asleep and if it's uncomfortable, well, overcoming pain is all part of some styles of meditation. But not the meditation for happiness I'm teaching here. You don't want to be distracted by thinking how painful your ankles or knees are.

I would suggest you try one or more of the following:

▶ Sit cross-legged with a cushion supporting the rear of your buttocks and keeping your spine straight. Rest your hands on your knees. One way is with the palms up and the thumb and forefinger of each hand touching to form an 'O'.

▶ Sit on a dining-type chair, with your spine straight and not against the back of the seat. Just place your hands, palms down, lightly on your knees.

▶ Lie down. Many teachers frown on this as not being 'proper' and because of the danger of falling asleep. But, in fact, it's an excellent position for meditating because it automatically reduces beta waves. As with the other positions, the spine should be straight, so lie on your back with your arms by your sides, palms up, and your feet shoulder width apart. To overcome the danger of falling asleep, try lying on the floor rather than the bed so you don't get too comfortable.

Insight

You could meditate all day. But, in the context of a busy modern life 20–30 minutes is the sort of thing to aim for. The longer you can devote to it, the more likely you are to reach a deep state. Nevertheless, even a few minutes' meditation is better than nothing. And sometimes it's possible to experience a meditative state while doing other things, such as walking or running. However long the session, the benefits ripple out far beyond it. Some people like to set a timer. This can work well because it removes any anxiety about not meditating for long enough or, on the other hand, taking too long and being late for the next thing you have to do. But others prefer to let whatever happens happen.

MEDITATING FOR HAPPINESS

So you're sitting or lying down. Then what? Different people use different techniques and again you need to experiment to find out what works best for you. Some people, for example, stare at a candle flame or an image or a wall, others repeat mantras; still others repeat small almost imperceptible gestures.

Here's a simple way of meditating for happiness that works.

1 Sitting or lying down with your eyes closed, notice your breathing.
2 Without forcing anything, gradually slow down your breathing.
3 Make your exhalations longer than your inhalations.
4 Empty your mind of any thoughts of past or future.
5 Just concentrate on experiencing the present moment, which is your breath.
6 If any thoughts push their way into your mind, just let them drift past; don't pursue them.
7 When your breathing is slow and relaxed, notice your heartbeat.
8 Without forcing anything, gradually try to think it slower.
9 Next notice the sound of your blood flowing in your ears.
10 Without forcing anything, gradually try to think it slower.
11 In the same way, visit any other parts of your body that you choose.
12 Now notice the little dots that 'illuminate' the blackness of your closed eyes.
13 Imagine the dots are stars and that you're floating in an immense space inside your own body.
14 Relax your jaw and let your mouth open into a smile.
15 Continue like this as long as you like.

Self-coaching tips

▶ If you can't seem to get into a meditative state at all, try lying on the floor rather than sitting.
▶ Try touching the tip of your ring finger against the fleshy base of your thumb as you breathe in and moving it away as you breathe out. As you breathe in, think 'so' and as you breathe out, think 'hum' – it's a classic mantra.

> ▶ Gradually slow down your breathing, making your exhalation longer than your inhalation.
> ▶ Let your mouth fall open and your tongue relax completely and drop out.

AM I MEDITATING?

Beginners often wonder if they're meditating correctly or even at all. What should it feel like? In fact, there is no precise definition but the stages of increasingly deeper and deeper meditation should go something like this:

▶ **Stage 1** – Your mind is no longer filled with everyday matters and you sense that you're drifting towards sleep; you're on the very fringe of the meditative state.
▶ **Stage 2** – As you go deeper, images may come at you from nowhere. You don't actually fall asleep but start to feel as if you're floating. You may feel like rocking and swaying; that's fine at this stage but you'll need to stop moving to go deeper.
▶ **Stage 3** – You become intensely aware of the functioning of your body – breathing, heartbeat, blood flow – but at the same time you no longer know where your body ends and other things begin. Parts of your body may feel very heavy.
▶ **Stage 4** – You feel 'spaced out' and quite detached but, at the same time, alert.
▶ **Stage 5** – You feel in touch with the universe and nothing else matters at all.

The deepest meditative states are usually only reached by those who have been practising for a long time – perhaps two or three years. But you may occasionally experience moments of those deeper states even as a beginner.

Insight

Remember that meditation is not a competition. Every experience of meditation is slightly different. Don't set out with a goal and then consider the session a failure because you didn't achieve it. Just experience and enjoy whatever occurs.

Dual techniques

I call these next ones 'dual techniques' because they tackle internal and external happiness simultaneously. You enjoy doing them just for themselves but, at the same time, they can bring about profound changes inside.

The happiness exercise

I'm now going to give you an exercise that's proven beyond any doubt to increase happiness.

It's so powerful that, in the UK, the National Institute for Health and Clinical Excellence (NICE) recommends it (together with psychotherapy) in preference to antidepressants as the first line of treatment for mild depression.

The exercise is...exercise.

If you're one of those people who hates the idea of exertion, then I suggest you go to the nearest sports centre and watch the faces of people throwing themselves into the swimming pool, or whacking a squash ball around, or bouncing on a trampoline. Huge numbers of people derive immense pleasure from taking part in all kinds of physical activities, without even giving a thought to the amazing effect it's all having on their personalities. The astonishing truth is that building up to a regular routine of physical exercise could, indeed, change the way you think, feel and behave.

Our ancestors had to be capable of vigorous activity if they were to eat. When their muscles screamed for respite, those whose bodies produced chemicals to ease the pain were the ones who ran down the prey and got the food. Logically, they were also the ones evolution selected. Well, that's a simplistic way of putting it but right in essence. Nowadays we only have to be capable of lifting a can off a shelf but our bodies remain unchanged. So if we want to enjoy the same chemicals that gave our ancestors endurance, relief from pain, courage, self-belief, optimism, exhilaration and happiness, we have to exercise. Here are some of those chemicals:

▶ **Endorphins** – the word means 'endogenous morphine', that's to say, morphine-like substances produced by the body. Endorphins combat pain, promote happiness and are one of the ingredients in the 'runner's high'.

- ▶ **Phenylethylamine (PEA)** – this chemical is also found in chocolate as well as some fizzy drinks. Researchers at Rush University and the Center for Creative Development, Chicago, have demonstrated that PEA is a powerful antidepressant. Meanwhile, scientists at Nottingham Trent University in the UK have shown that PEA levels increase significantly following exercise.
- ▶ **Noradrenaline/norepinephrine (NE)** – when generated by exercise, noradrenaline tends to make you feel happy, confident, positive and expansive.
- ▶ **Serotonin** – the link with exercise isn't so strong for this one, but serotonin is a neurotransmitter for happiness and there's reason to think exercise elevates its level in the brain.

In addition, exercise lowers the level of:

- ▶ **Cortisol** – a stress hormone, cortisol is linked with low mood.

There are also two further processes at work:

- ▶ **Thermogenics** – exercise increases the body's core temperature, which in turn relaxes muscles, which in turn induces a feeling of tranquility.
- ▶ **Right-brain/Left-brain** – repetitive physical activities, such as jogging, 'shut down' the left side of the brain (logical thought), freeing up the right-brain (creative thought). It's a kind of meditation and it's why solutions to seemingly intractable problems often appear 'by magic' when exercising.

HOW MUCH EXERCISE?

Remember that we're primarily looking at exercise as a source of happiness, not physical fitness. So how much exercise does it take to boost those all-important happiness chemicals? The good news is, surprisingly little. Let's take a look:

- ▶ **Endorphins** – the level of beta-endorphins, the chemicals the body releases to combat pain, increases by five times after 12 minutes of vigorous exercise.
- ▶ **Phenylethylamine (PEA)** – the researchers at Nottingham Trent University found that running at 70 per cent of maximum heart

rate (MHR – see below) for 30 minutes increased the level of phenylacetic acid in the urine (which reflects phenylethylamine) by 77 per cent.

▶ **Noradrenaline/norepinephrine (NE)** – this increases by up to ten times following eight minutes of vigorous exercise.

Self-coaching tip

It would seem that around ten minutes of vigorous exercise is already highly beneficial in terms of endorphins and NE but that PEA levels are slower to augment. The minimum for a significant personality effect is probably 20 minutes of brisk exercise three times a week (and you'll need to allow five minutes at either end for warming up and cooling down). Five times a week would be better. Longer sessions, within reason, would be better still. Dr James Blumenthal carried out a study on 150 depressed people, aged 50 or over, at Duke University in 1999. Not only did exercise substantially improve mood, Dr Blumenthal concluded that for each 50-minute increment of exercise, there was an accompanying 50 per cent reduction in relapse rate. So even a little is good but more is better (within reason).

Warning
Health professionals warn that if you haven't been exercising regularly and have any of the following characteristics, you should check with your doctor before beginning an exercise programme:

▶ over 35 and a smoker
▶ over 40 and inactive
▶ diabetic
▶ at risk of heart disease
▶ high blood pressure
▶ high cholesterol
▶ experience chest pains while exercising
▶ difficulty breathing during mild exertion.

WHAT KIND OF EXERCISE?
Steady rhythmical exercise seems to be better than the stop/start sort of exercise you might get in, say, cricket. But any exercise is better than no exercise. The important thing is to find an activity or

activities you really enjoy and can do several times a week all year round. There are so many possibilities nowadays that just about everyone should be able to find something that's fun. If you're very resistant to the whole idea of exercise, it's all the more important to find an activity that really inspires you. Adding a goal, other than 'happy-fitness', can help. For example, rather than swim up and down in a pool, you might set yourself the target of swimming a whole stretch of coastline bit by bit, getting to know all the various bays. Or you could sign up for races. Or what about raising money for charity through sponsored activities? Keeping an exercise diary is also a good idea, so you can monitor your progress and take pride in your achievements.

Food for thought

If you like eating, you're really going to like this one. It's eating yourself happy. The general principle is this. You can only eat so much in a day, so make sure it's nutritious – that's to say, contains all the vitamins and minerals necessary for a healthy mind (and a healthy body). Deficiency can directly cause low moods and even depression.

There are 'empty calories' that contain very few vitamins and minerals (sweets, crisps, 'junk food') and, on the other hand, there are calories that come packed together with vitamins and minerals. So do your best to restrict those empty calories. In order to make sure you're getting enough of the nutrients for health and happiness, your diet each day should include the following (a cup is 250 ml):

▶ whole grains, such as rice, barley and wholemeal bread, as the foundation of at least one meal
▶ vegetables, including green leafy vegetables (about four cups)
▶ fruit (about four cups)
▶ nuts, seeds and legumes (about one cup).

There isn't space here to detail all the beneficial foods but, in brief, here are some that are almost 'food pharmaceuticals':

▶ **Brazil nuts** – many people are selenium deficient, which results in low moods. Half a dozen ready-shelled Brazil nuts per day will put that right.

- ▶ **Caffeine** – a cup of real coffee in the morning and another in the afternoon will keep up your mental energy (double the dose for tea). But be aware that caffeine makes some people feel anxious.
- ▶ **Chilli peppers** – the 'burning' sensation can trick your body into producing endorphins, the body's natural painkillers.
- ▶ **Chocolate** – contains a veritable cocktail of 'happy chemicals', but watch out for the calories.
- ▶ **Folic acid (folate)** – deficiency causes levels of serotonin, a 'happiness neurotransmitter' to plummet. To get more, eat green leafy vegetables, beans and peas.
- ▶ **Garlic** – boosts mood, reduces anxiety, irritability and fatigue, and increases the male sex drive.
- ▶ **Saw palmetto** – taken as a supplement, increases the availability of testosterone, helping older men to feel more positive – and sexy.
- ▶ **Wheatgerm** – contains tyrosine from which dopamine, one of the 'happiness neurotransmitters', can be synthesized.
- ▶ **Zinc** – deficiency causes depression. Only oysters are rich enough in zinc to guarantee an adequate intake, otherwise take a supplement.

You also need to pay particular attention to the kind of fat in your diet.

Minimize:

- ▶ **trans-fatty acids** – which are in lamb, beef, dairy products and margarine (which means cakes and biscuits as well)
- ▶ **saturated fats** – which are mostly in animal products
- ▶ **omega-6 polyunsaturated fatty acids (PUFAs)** – which are found in animal products and vegetable oils.

Maximize:

- ▶ **monounsaturated fats** – such as olive oil
- ▶ **omega-3 polyunsaturated fatty acids (PUFAs)** – found in oily fish, rapeseed (canola), soy, walnut and flaxseed oils.

About two-thirds of the human brain by weight, and about 75 per cent of the myelin sheath that surrounds nerves, is made up of polyunsaturated fatty acids. The key difference between omega-6s and omega-3s is this:

- ▶ Omega-6s cause inflammation, constrict blood vessels, encourage blood platelets to stick together, form rigid cell membranes and release free radicals, which destroy cells.
- ▶ Omega-3s reduce inflammation, dilate blood vessels, deter blood platelets from sticking together and form flexible cell membranes.

For optimum brain functioning, including happiness, you want flexible cell membranes, that is, omega-3s. But in the modern diet, omega-6s tend to outweigh omega-3s ten times over. Although omega-6s are still essential, this ratio is bad. What you actually need to do is to aim for more omega-3s than omega-6s.

Insight

Flaxseed is the only known non-fish oil that provides more omega-3s than omega-6s. In other words, if you don't eat fish, try to use flaxseed oil as often as possible. When you can't use flaxseed oil use olive oil, which is only 8 per cent omega-6.

Self-coaching tip

It's a common error to think that alcohol 'cheers you up'. Its action is actually rather complicated. It does have the ability to prolong the effect of dopamine, a 'happiness neurotransmitter' but if you're feeling down when you drink, alcohol is more likely to make you feel worse. In fact, it is a neurotoxin. It also lowers the level of oxytocin, a hormone that enhances the sense of touch and the pleasure of cuddling and sex. The advice is to drink very moderately or not at all.

External happiness

In the West, we tend to feel guilty about enjoying ourselves. We know there are so many people living in appalling conditions. Being happy can seem like callousness. But that's not logical. Your unhappiness cannot possibly help other people. In fact, the reverse. Happy people are far more likely to help others than unhappy people. When you're unhappy, you feel demoralized. When you feel happy, you're positive and optimistic and ready to tackle problems. At the same time, your happiness is infectious. People around you will sense it and feel happier too.

So never feel guilty about enjoying all the wonderful things planet Earth and the society of other human beings can offer.

The next question is: how? Well, I can't tell you what to enjoy. The best I can do is pass on this piece of advice from the Norwegian philosopher Arne Naess. Ask yourself:

▶ In what situation do I experience the maximum satisfaction of my whole being?

When you know the answer to that, you know where to find external happiness. If you haven't yet discovered the answer, keep on trying lots of different possibilities.

Things or experiences?

People often ask if there's a connection between money and happiness. We like to believe there isn't or, even better, that wealthy people are miserable. The truth is that, in our society anyway, wealthy people do tend to be happier than everyone else. Sorry! But there it is. (Although there are plenty of unhappy rich people, too.)

That's the bad news. The good news is that they're only a little bit happier than people who are reasonably well off.

When you think about it, it's a fairly pointless question anyway, except from the academic viewpoint. If you're wealthy, you're probably not going to give your money away if I tell you that poor people are happier. And if you are poor, how exactly do you intend to get rich if I tell you wealthy people are happier?

It reality it works like this. If you're too poor to pay the bills and enjoy a few of life's purchasable pleasures, then a modest increase in your income (in monetary terms) could have quite a dramatic effect on your happiness. But once you have enough money to be 'comfortable', then any further increase won't achieve very much.

Just as drug addicts need bigger and bigger doses, so people who have become wealthy seem to need increasingly expensive products to derive the same level of satisfaction they'd once gained from cheaper ones. Even just *thinking* about money seems to destroy the pleasure of simple things, as demonstrated by a team at the University of British Columbia. Volunteers were asked to taste chocolate. But before doing so they were asked to fill in one of two versions of a simple questionnaire, one containing a photo of Canadian dollars and one containing a neutral picture. Apparently, the 'dollars' group spent less time eating the chocolate and enjoyed it less.

But Elizabeth Dunn, a social psychologist and assistant professor at the University of British Columbia, points out that just because money fails to buy some people happiness doesn't prove that it can't ever buy happiness. The problem, she says, is that people have a natural tendency to want to buy *things* so as to gain status and impress the Jones's, whereas they should be buying *experiences*.

Professor Ryan Howell, a psychologist at San Francisco State University, has the figures to prove it. He led a study which showed that money spent on experiences brought more lasting happiness than money spent on material possessions. The reason is that experiences leave happy memories, which can be cherished over the years, whereas most consumer goods soon wear out.

Insight

Memories, too, can fade. In my experience, it's important for the experiences to be strong ones that will be unlikely to be forgotten. Revisit your favourite memories regularly to keep them sharp.

Self-coaching tip

Make a point of having at least one special experience every day. They don't necessarily have to cost anything at all. It could be a special meal together with candles. It could be a game of hide-and-seek with your children. You could hike or swim or cycle at a beauty spot. You could discover a new piece of music. You could make love in a new place or a new position. When you do these things, record them in some way so you'll never forget:

▶ Write about them in your diary.
▶ Take a still photo or make a video.
▶ Make an entry on your social networking site.

Depression

Statistics show that people high in Neuroticism are not only liable to more depression than others, they actually do endure more negative life events. It's not difficult to see why this might be the case. Constant worrying increases the risk of certain illnesses. Attempts to reduce anguish may be self-destructive (alcohol and other drugs, risk-taking). And highly Neurotic people are difficult to live with, increasing the likelihood that relationships will disintegrate and the sufferer be left with no support.

Many psychologists now see depression as an ongoing condition, which becomes acute from time to time. A person who has suffered from depression has a 50 per cent chance of suffering again within two years and an 80 per cent chance of suffering another bout during their lifetime. That suggests a genetic component and, indeed, experiments have confirmed it (see Chapter 10). Psychologists say that people who suffer from depression think and behave slightly differently when compared with people who never suffer depression. This tends to make depression something of a circular problem.

So it's very important to break into that circle at the earliest opportunity. The longer depression goes on, the more the brain is reshaped as a 'depressed brain' and the harder it is to change. If you suffer from a low mood that just won't go away, seek professional help promptly.

10 TIPS FOR SUCCESS

1 Seek out both internal and external happiness, not one or the other.

2 Cultivate the mindset 'I'm all right and you're all right'.

3 Don't let the lid off your anger; turn the heat down.

4 Make a list of the things you worry about and compare it with the bad things that actually happened – there's the proof that you're worrying unnecessarily.

5 Meditation tends to increase activity in the frontal lobe of the left-brain – the part associated with higher moods and optimism.

6 Exercise increases the level of 'happy neurotransmitters' in the brain.

7 Deficiency of key vitamins and minerals can cause low moods and depression – eating enough will restore happiness.

8 Ask yourself: in what situation do I experience the maximum satisfaction of my whole being? Then go for that situation.

9 In the long term, experiences produce more happiness than consumer goods.

10 Seek professional help as soon as a low mood becomes prolonged.

10

What made your personality?

In this chapter you will learn:
- *how you're born with a personality*
- *how genes play a major role in making you special*
- *why your upbringing didn't make much difference.*

This book is all about the real you. It's about discovering who you are, why you are, and what you can achieve.

But is there any such thing as the 'real' anybody? Aren't we all just the products of outside forces that arbitrarily shaped us in particular ways – our parents, our siblings, our schoolteachers, accidents that occurred, right or wrong places we happened to be in at the wrong or right times?

The science of personality has reached a point at which we can answer that question emphatically. No one is born a blank slate. Part of you is inscribed into that slate so deeply that nothing can change it. In other words, a big part of your personality is inherited, passed on to you through your genes.

The incredible twins

Let me tell you about James Springer and James Lewis. James Springer was an average guy. He was divorced and had remarried. His first wife was called Linda and his second wife was called Betty. His first son was called James Allan. He'd had police training and still worked part-time in law enforcement. He'd had a dog called Toy. He chained-smoked Salem cigarettes. And he had the annoying habit of chewing his fingernails right down. Nothing very extraordinary, then. Not, that is, until he discovered he had a twin brother from whom he'd been separated a few weeks after birth.

His twin brother was called James Lewis. James Lewis was also on his second marriage. His first had been to a woman called Linda and his second to a woman called Betty. He'd called his first son James Alan. James Lewis had also had police training. He'd also owned a dog called Toy. He also chained-smoked Salem cigarettes. And he, too, chewed his fingernails.

The word that comes to mind is 'spooky'. We're not just talking about identical twins having similar personalities even though they were raised apart. That's easy to believe. We're also talking about similar life events. It's as if Fate had already planned the life of a boy called Jim and that when that zygote (fertilized egg) unexpectedly split in half (for once taking Fate by surprise), so both boys were obliged to live two near-identical life stories. When James Springer and James Lewis married, remarried, chose names for their dogs and applied for jobs they thought they were making conscious *free* decisions. But were they?

Of course, not all twins separated as babies have so many incredible things in common as James Springer and James Lewis. And research has sometimes been muddied by twins who have deliberately concocted their life stories to gain attention and money, and even by scientists who have tampered with data to make it fit their pet theories. Even so, the remarkable, verified stories of hundreds of identical twins separated at birth prove that many of our personality traits are programmed by our genes. The *real you* is in your genes. If you want to be true to yourself, that means being true to your genes.

What is a gene?

A gene used to be described as 'the basic unit of heredity'. Now things have got a lot more complicated. A more up-to-date definition is: 'a union of genomic sequences encoding a coherent set of potentially overlapping functional products'. So that's clear then! For our purposes I think we can stick with 'the basic unit of heredity'. That's good enough.

Something else that's changed in recent years is the idea that for each characteristic (hair colour, Extroversion, Openness, etc.) you received one gene from your mother and one from your father.

The new thinking is that everybody has every gene and what distinguishes one person from another is that these genes can have slightly different versions known as alleles. Again, for our purposes, that doesn't really change very much.

As for a genome, that can be seen as the total complement of genes in an organism or cell – because every cell (with minor exceptions) contains a complete set of genes for making you *you*. Richard Dawkins gives as an analogy that the nucleus of every cell is a bookcase containing the architectural plans for that body, and that the plans (for humans) come in 46 volumes called chromosomes. Each page of every volume would then be a gene, detailing some aspect of the body, brain or personality.

The 46 volumes (chromosomes) are in pairs, so that 23 come from your father and 23 come from your mother. To simplify things, let's say your father supplies volumes 1F up to 23F and your mother 1M up to 23M. In that case, page 5 of volume 3F will correspond with page 5 in volume 3M, that's to say, will give instructions about the same thing. If both pages carry identical instructions, that's the way you'll be. If they carry different instructions, there are two possibilities. Either one gene beats the other (in more technical language, one gene is dominant and the other is recessive). Or a compromise is reached between the two.

Where does the famous DNA (deoxyribonucleic acid) come into the picture? That's what genes are made of. DNA molecules are too small to be seen even through microscopes, but it's been worked out that each one consists of two chains of even smaller molecules called nucleotides, twisted together into what is the now iconic 'double helix'.

There are only four kinds of these nucleotides – A (adenine), T (thymine), C (cytosine) and G (guanine) – and everything that lives, from a blade of grass to a human, contains the same ones. The only thing that differs from one species to another, and from one individual to the next, is the sequence of those four different kinds of nucleotides. In effect, the instructions for making not only your body but also a large chunk of your personality are written in a code using the four letters A, T, C and G (just as everything in a computer is written in a code of 1 or 0).

There's an awful lot we still don't know about genes. In particular, we still don't know exactly how we get from a single cell (containing the master set of 46 volumes) to the complicated thing that is a body.

But here's something important that we do know:

▶ Genes can survive unchanged for millions of years.

Just think about what it means. The roots of your personality lie in an environment very different from today's. That's why, as we saw in Chapter 3, men are programmed to try to have sex with as many partners as possible, and women are programmed to refuse all but those who will father and help raise the fittest offspring.

If we weren't able to control these primitive inclinations, we'd probably be in a lot of trouble. But nowadays we're not entirely stuck with the physical selves our genes have created and we're certainly not puppets when it comes to behaviour either.

The question is, to what extent do these 'primitive' genes control our personalities and therefore our behavior, and to what extent can we modify or improve matters through upbringing, education and so on?

HOW MUCH IS HERITABLE?

Scientists are still arguing about this. The idea that babies are born with personalities has such important social and political implications that emotions can run very high. But I side with those who argue that about half the variation in personality is heritable (as well as half the variation in intelligence and life outcomes).

Insight

At first it can be rather hard to get your head around this idea of such-and-such a proportion of the 'variation in personality'. The point is that (with very rare exceptions) all human beings have what might be called a 'basic personality structure' just as all human beings have two arms, two legs, and so on. The scientists aren't so interested in that. They want to know why Fred can't control his impulses but Sue can. So it's the differences between people that they focus on.

Here are some of the specific personality traits that we know can be passed on genetically:

- ▶ The Big Five personality traits
- ▶ General intelligence
- ▶ Language skills
- ▶ Religiosity
- ▶ Political outlook
- ▶ Drug and alcohol dependence
- ▶ Gambling
- ▶ Sex drive
- ▶ Likelihood of divorce
- ▶ Likelihood of depression
- ▶ Hours spent watching television
- ▶ Selective mutism (difficulty speaking in public)
- ▶ Sensitivity to bitter tastes/preference for sweet tastes.

How did the scientists come to these conclusions? Largely by twins studies. It's possible to compare identical twins separated at birth. It's also possible to compare identical twins raised together with fraternal twins raised together. A third technique is to compare biological siblings with adopted siblings.

Insight

None of these methods is perfect and various objections have been raised as to their validity. One is that while certain traits may correlate with genes, that does not in itself prove that the genes caused them. In Chapter 5 we saw that tall attractive men and women earned more on average than their shorter, less attractive colleagues. Careless researchers might therefore conclude they've discovered genes for financial success when, in fact, they've discovered genes for height and good looks, which only indirectly cause financial success.

If we look at high Neuroticism, for example, which was long ago proclaimed by personality specialist Hans Eysenck to be 'to a large extent hereditarily determined', we now know that one of the mechanisms lies in the so-called COMT gene alleles Val158 and Met158. Roughly half the population has one copy of each, a quarter have two copies of Val158 and a quarter have two copies of Met158. In experiments, those carrying two copies of Met158 were more easily startled than the others and tended to be more anxious. (Curiously, the COMT gene is also linked to brain ageing – those with the Met variant tended to perform better when younger but their mental function declined more rapidly with age, compared to those with the Val variant who performed less well when younger but who declined far more slowly with age.)

Similarly, there are two versions of the serotonin transporter gene 5-HTTLPR (which removes serotonin from the synapses between neurons), a short version and a long version. Some people have two copies of the short version, some have two copies of the long version and some have one of each. In a study headed by Avshalom Caspi, a group of New Zealanders was interviewed to determine how many negative life events they had suffered in five years – that's to say, things such as the death of someone close, divorce, serious ill health, and so on. The long/long group had rates of depression under 20 per cent, even when four or more negative life events had occurred. By contrast, the short/short group had a depression rate of 40 per cent with four or more negative life events, and 30 per cent with three. The short/long group lay somewhere in between.

Even the likelihood of holding religious beliefs or not could have a genetic element. A religious tendency was shown to be heritable via twins studies conducted by geneticists Lindon Eaves and Nicholas Martin, and a candidate gene, VMAT2, has been identified by fellow geneticist Dean Hamer. (Specific religious beliefs, however, are not heritable but would come under the category 'memes', a term coined by Richard Dawkins to mean an idea, behaviour or style that spreads from one person to another by imitation within a culture.)

In his book *The God Gene: How Faith Is Hardwired Into Our Genes*, Hamer claims that VMAT2 acts by altering monoamine levels. Monoamines are neurotransmitters, including dopamine, adrenaline (epinephrine), noradrenaline (norepinephrine), and serotonin. As to why a spiritual tendency would be favoured by natural selection, Hamer argues that by making people feel more optimistic it would give them a survival advantage.

Of course, a 'god gene' wouldn't in itself prove anything about the existence of God, one way or the other. But it would help explain why people would believe in God, without evidence.

CAN YOU MODIFY YOUR GENES?

What genes don't contain is any knowledge, skill, or wisdom acquired by the creature they're in during its lifetime. In other words, your father's acquired wisdom that being faithful to your mother brought him more happiness than sleeping around, couldn't be passed on to you genetically (although he might have passed it on to you verbally or by example). Likewise, your father couldn't benefit genetically from the acquired wisdom of your paternal grandparents. And so on and so on. Nothing you do to improve yourself prior to conceiving your own children can be passed on to them through your genes.

But the idea that your genetic blueprint, those 23 pairs of 'volumes', can never naturally be modified in any way, is changing. And a lot of that is due to Mario Fraga and Manel Esteller of the Spanish National Cancer Centre in Madrid. They discovered there are already tiny differences between 'identical' twin foetuses, and that the differences accumulate as the years go by, especially when twins are raised apart. The theory is that the genetic aspect of your personality is not entirely due to which genes you've inherited, but to which of the thousands of genes are active at any given time and which are dormant. Fraga and Esteller found that genes could be deactivated by a process known as DNA methylation, while dormant genes could be turned on by a process called acetylation. These processes don't happen in the same way in each twin.

The implications of this are enormous. If we could find a way of harnessing methylation and acetylation, more powerful ways of changing personality could become possible. Given that it was only in 2001 that the complete sequence of the human genome was published, research is still in its very early days. Meanwhile, we'll be looking at ways you can change your personality right now in Chapters 12 and 13.

The other half

So your genes account for about half the variation in your personality. What about the other half? Quite likely you're thinking that it's mostly the result of your upbringing. That's to say, your home life, your neighbourhood, the way your parents were, the ideals and beliefs they instilled in you and so on. If that *is* what you're thinking, then you're in line with most people and especially most of those parents who spend their lives running little Jimmy and little Janey to their extra-curricular activities. But you're completely at odds with most psychologists. The prevailing scientific opinion is that parenting counts for very little when it comes to the variation in personality, intelligence and life outcomes. Some specialists go even further and place the influence of parents at approximately...zero.

That's right. Zero!

THE SHARED ENVIRONMENT VERSUS THE UNIQUE ENVIRONMENT

The awkward thing for advocates of conscientious parenting is this: if parenting counts for very much, then children growing up with one set of parents should be more alike than children growing up with another set of parents. But they're not. Siblings who grow up together in a family are no more alike than siblings separated at birth. Adopted siblings are no more similar than children selected at random. All of this is beyond dispute.

It was back in 1987 that geneticist Robert Plomin and child specialist Denise Daniels published an article called 'Why Are Children In The Same Family So Different From One Another?' The academic community began to get interested. Various studies, articles and books followed. Huge publicity came in 1998 when Judith Rich Harris, also a child development specialist, published *The Nurture Assumption*. Reviewing all the evidence in his 2002 book, *The Blank Slate*, Steven Pinker, a bestselling author and Johnstone Professor of Psychology at Harvard University, wrote that 'whatever experiences siblings share by growing up in the same home makes little or no difference in the kind of people they turn out to be'. Many ambitious parents were outraged. Instinctively they believed that what they were doing must make a substantial difference. But the 'Zeroists' have stuck to their guns.

How, then, do they explain 'the other half'? The Zeroists distinguish between two kinds of environmental influence:

▶ the shared environment
▶ the unique environment.

The shared environment (or the 'family environment') comprises the kinds of things I've just mentioned that act more or less equally on siblings. The unique environment comprises all the things that are particular to each child – being the favourite or not, having a particular illness at a particular age, being bullied at school and so on.

It's the unique environment that, the Zeroists argue, accounts for just about everything after genes have been taken into account, while the shared environment accounts for almost nothing at all.

Here's why I think they've overstated their case.

The strange story of László Polgár

The Hungarian chess teacher László Polgár is a very unusual man. Convinced that geniuses are made, not born, he wrote a book called *Bring Up Genius* and then set about proving that he was right. First he had to find a woman who would agree to help him in his experiment. Klara, a schoolteacher who lived in a Hungarian-speaking enclave in Ukraine, fitted his needs. He married her, brought her home to Hungary and set about his experiment. His first subject, Zsuzsa, was born in 1969. Zsófia followed in 1974 and Judit two years later.

The girls were educated at home in various subjects but especially chess. So how did they make out? In 1984, at the age of 15, Zsuzsa became the highest ranked female chess player in the world and in 1991, at the age of 21, was the first woman to become a Grandmaster. To put that into context, there are slightly fewer than a thousand Grandmasters in the world (once gained, the title is never lost) and only about a dozen are women. Judit followed as a Grandmaster later that year at the age of only 15. Zsófia is an International Master, one rank below Grandmaster, but, even so, putting her in the top 0.25% of all tournament players.

Three daughters. Three successes. Three chess geniuses.

The Polgár experience is unusual but far from unique.

Boris Sidis (1867–1923), a doctor, psychologist and psychiatrist, was another who deliberately set out to raise a genius. His son William James Sidis (1898–1944) could read the *New York Times* at age 18 months and speak eight languages at age eight. In 1909, at the age of 11, he became the youngest person to enter Harvard, began lecturing the following year and was awarded his Bachelor of Arts at the age of 16. And it's not just a case of intellectual development. Other parents have facilitated very different kinds of achievements. Cleopatra Stratan, the daughter of Moldovan-Romanian singer Pavel

Stratan, was earning one thousand euros a song at the age of three. Willie Mosconi, the son of a pool hall owner, became a professional billiards player at the age of six. And the Williams sisters, who have both ranked No.1 in the world in women's tennis daughters, are the daughters of Richard Williams, the tennis equivalent of László Polgár.

Of course, it's possible to argue that the Polgárs all inherited genes that were conducive to chess success. But there's a lot more to chess than being able to see a few moves ahead. You have to have good spatial awareness (something in which girls are, on average, naturally less able than boys). You have to be comfortable playing in public (high Extroversion would help). You have to be able to withstand the mental pressure (low Neuroticism would help). You have to have the drive (high Conscientiousness would help). It seems almost impossible that all three girls could have inherited the entire package.

Anders Ericsson, a professor of psychology at Florida State University, agrees. Having spent 20 years studying geniuses, he concluded that 'extended, deliberate practice' was the key. He found, for example, that the finest pianists and violinists had spent 10,000 hours practising by the age of 20, about double that spent by other good but not outstanding players. In only a few instances did Ericsson conclude that it was essential to be born with the necessary aptitudes – height, for example, is essential for basketball players as well as swimmers.

The Zeroists' answer is that skills and accomplishments are quite different to personality. They never have denied that these things can be taught. That much is true, But it's very difficult to argue that you can mould children in terms of chess, or languages, or tennis and yet not influence, say, how open they are to new ideas, or with how much confidence they conduct themselves, or how well they handle problems. It doesn't seem to add up.

My explanation is this. Studies into the shared environment deal with average sorts of situations. When twins are up for adoption in separate households, the successful adoptive parents are not those who plan to use the infant as an experiment in specialization, nor, of course, to abuse him or her in any way. Adoptive parents are, by and large, middle-class people with fairly similar views.

Although the separated twins studied were often brought up in households that were different, they weren't *that* different. In the majority of cases, the adoptive parents, who had been screened for their suitability, wanted children, loved them, believed in the value of education and provided at least reasonable standards of comfort and care. What would have been the impact if one separated twin had never received any love, never been sent to school, been subjected to sexual abuse, or been made an accomplice in the step-parents' criminal activities?

I have a further problem with the Zero argument. What would be the mechanism by which the unique environment could affect a child's personality when the shared environment could not? For example, if sibling A falls off his bicycle (unique environment), then that may well have an impact on his personality. However, if both sibling A and sibling B fall off their bicycles, there won't be any effect on personality (shared environment).

This seems somewhat preposterous. Admittedly I have chosen a rather unscientific example to make a point, but the point remains.

GROUP SOCIALIZATION THEORY

The child expert Judith Rich Harris has put forward the theory that the biggest aspect of the unique environment is the peer group – the children you played with, the children your children play with. She calls this Group Socialization theory. One clue that this is correct comes from the fact that children almost always copy the accents of their peers, rather than their parents. Thus couples who move to a new and different area and then have children will find them speaking like the locals.

Children want status among their peers. This is why some teenagers take up smoking even if their parents don't, indulge in risky behaviour and even break the law. Parents often try to explain away bad behaviour by saying, 'He/she got in with the wrong kind of children and was led astray.' Instinctively we all know the importance of Group Socialization. Judges have heard the excuse many times but that's not to say it's invalid.

To what extent, though, is it really correct to put the peer group under the heading 'unique environment'. Yes, each child in a family usually has his or her own friends. But very often those friends are drawn from the same social milieu. And even if we do classify friends as 'unique', does it mean that parents have nothing to do with it?

Many parents move houses precisely so their children can mix with others of a certain type. Some send their children to boarding schools to guarantee it. They choose after-school activities on the basis of the kinds of children they attract. And they discourage some friends while inviting others to come on holiday.

Self-coaching tip

If you're a parent, one of the most effective things you can do is to make sure your children mix with others who exhibit the kinds of tendencies you value and who don't smoke, drink, take drugs, or indulge in criminal activity.

THE BLISSFUL WOMB

There's an important environment we haven't discussed yet. That's the environment you experienced for nine months before you were even born, inside the womb and inside the birth canal.

Let's first of all tackle the issue of whether or not anyone can actually remember that far back at all. In humans there's a mechanism known as 'infantile amnesia', meaning that adults remember little or nothing of their infant years. The average age from which memories survive seems to be around three years and six months but there's fairly persuasive evidence that no small number of adults can remember things that happened when they were as young as two.

Researchers at Memorial University of Newfoundland found that children aged four and five could recall things that happened to them when they were around 18 months. But when the same children were interviewed two years later, those memories could no longer be recalled, even when the children were given prompts.

Various explanations have been offered for infantile amnesia. Freud favoured the idea that it was essential for the repression of traumatic psychosexual development that would otherwise be damaging. Many scientists, however, believe infants lack the necessary neurological development, especially of the hippocampus and prefrontal cortex, for the creation of long-term autobiographical memories. Lack of language, as well as a postulated lack of self-awareness until the age of two, are also advanced as possible factors.

But the fact that you can't remember something doesn't mean it doesn't have an effect on you. It's very easy to understand this in a physical context. For example, you may not be able to remember your hand being crushed when you were one year old but, nevertheless, your manual dexterity may have been reduced.

Dr Wendy Anne McCarty has reviewed more than 30 years of research and concludes that what she calls the 'primary period' – from 'preconception through the first year of postnatal life' – is vital to physical, emotional, mental, spiritual and relational wellbeing. She argues that experiences during the primary period lay down a blueprint for life.

It can seem a ridiculous idea at first but the more you think about it, the less ridiculous and the more plausible it seems. Let's turn it around. How could it be that a baby has thoughts on emerging from the birth canal but not beforehand? It seems to make no sense.

That the foetus remembers has been demonstrated in various experiments. There are three techniques:

▶ classical conditioning
▶ habituation
▶ exposure learning.

In classical conditioning, what is to become the conditioned stimulus (which normally evokes no response) is followed by an unconditioned stimulus (which normally does evoke a response). The usual way of doing this with a foetus is to use a vibration as the conditioned stimulus, followed by a loud noise as the unconditioned stimulus, causing the startled foetus to exhibit signs of anxiety by kicking. By the age of 32 weeks, and after just a dozen repetitions of the paired stimuli, some foetuses kick after receiving just the vibration, demonstrating that they have both remembered the vibration and learned that it means something unpleasant is about to happen.

Habituation involves directing a sound or vibration at a foetus until it stops reacting. That's to say, the foetus has become habituated. Habituation proves that the foetus has the ability to remember, otherwise it would always react as if it was the first time. Habituation to sound happens as early as 22 weeks. In a variation to this experiment, babies in the neonatal stage (the first 28 days after birth) that had been habituated in the womb were compared with those that hadn't been habituated. The babies that had been habituated needed fewer stimuli to again achieve habituation, proving that they had remembered what had happened in the womb some weeks earlier.

Exposure learning also involves subjecting the foetus to a stimulus in the womb and then checking the baby for signs of recognition. In one experiment, foetuses were exposed to the theme tune from the TV show *Neighbours*. As babies they were again played the tune and reacted by exhibiting various physiological changes, such as decreased heart rate, when a control group of other babies did not. Nor did other music have the same effect. Memory of the tune was strongest two to four days after birth but significantly diminished after 21 days. In another similar experiment, music by Debussy was played at times when mother and foetus were both tranquil. In the weeks following birth, the same music was played to various infants. Only those who had heard Debussy in the womb reacted by becoming more calm.

These, you might say, are rather trivial effects. But they establish a principle. And we also have evidence of far more dramatic things.

It was in 1962 that the world saw proof that drugs taken by an expectant mother could impact her developing baby. That was the year the first thalidomide babies were born. Till then it had been thought that the placenta acted as a barrier to prevent anything harmful passing from the mother's blood into the foetus. Thalidomide proved that was not so. Nor is thalidomide a particularly special case.

The foetus smokes if the mother smokes, with the result that the foetus receives less oxygen each time she lights up, lives in a state of anxiety and may go on to score high for Neuroticism. The foetus drinks alcohol if the mother drinks, and if the drinking is serious, may become an individual with memory problems, attention problems, lowered IQ and alcohol dependency.

These are things originating outside the mother. But why should chemicals originating inside be any different? It's easy to imagine that, say, a pregnant woman whose husband is violent will have more of the stress hormone cortisol circulating in her blood and that her foetus will, as a result, develop into a child who scores high for Neuroticism. There's plenty of anecdotal evidence for these kinds of effects but not so much hard scientific data. Certainly it's been demonstrated in rats that if the mother is stressed during pregnancy, her offspring are higher on the scale of Neuroticism than other rats. That's to say, they're slower to explore new environments and more cautious generally.

So not all wombs are equally blissful. And, in fact, none may be as blissful as we tend to think. It's been said that a far higher percentage of lives are lost in the womb than during the first fifty years of life on the outside. A lot of those spontaneous abortions may be due to problems with the foetus rather than the womb, but the fact remains that life in the womb is hazardous.

During the final three months, the womb becomes an increasingly cramped and uncomfortable place and the oxygen supply is frequently inadequate, causing hypoxia. Some scientists believe that, as a result, some foetuses suffer brain damage. So it may not be a question of the foetus being rudely expelled from its little paradise as much as it needing to escape if it is to survive. Which brings us to the birth experience.

A lot of cranky stuff has been written about being born. There's a whole industry in sorting out the psychological problems and personality quirks that are said to be birth-related. All kinds of things from claustrophobia to fear of sexual relations have been blamed on the minutes and hours spent in the birth canal. Nor is the Caesarean any kind of solution, according to this way of thinking, because it denies the baby the sensual skin contact it would have enjoyed in the vagina, as well as the sense of triumph on emerging into the world.

But stripping that all away (rightly or wrongly), we're still left with the incontrovertible fact that many babies have long and difficult births, and that they're strongly affected at the time, as proven by their highly elevated pulses. During labour oxygen starvation occurs. Some babies die. Why wouldn't that kind of trauma have some sort of an effect on personality?

Nevertheless, many psychologists argue that it doesn't. They can find no proof in, say, twins studies. But this is something that would be fiendishly difficult to prove anyway. Twins may seem to share the same environment but they don't. One is usually in a slightly more advantageous position than the other. One may have a better blood supply than the other. One may be bigger than the other (and probably dominant). And one twin has to be born before the other, so that the two birth experiences must be quite different.

> **Insight**
>
> It's been postulated that religious feelings are the result of life in the womb. The foetus has the sense of an omnipotent presence that is always there and on which it depends. Lloyd deMause of the Institute for Psychohistory ties it down specifically to the foetal relationship with the placenta, which supplies the oxygen and nutrients that make the foetus feel good. The search for 'oneness' is therefore seen as the desire to be reunited with the placenta, or the mother.

The last piece of the jigsaw

According to Dr Gary Marcus, Professor of Psychology at New York University, our genes are not blueprints that can specify every tiny detail of our bodies and brains. He sees them more as 'self-regulating recipes' which respond to environmental cues. Two dishes may be prepared in the same way with exactly the same quantities and cooked at the same temperature for the same length of time and yet they never turn out to be *exactly* the same. Maybe the courgettes in one dish were slightly more bitter than in the other. Maybe one pan had a trace of something on it. Maybe, by chance, something splashes into one pan but not the other.

Similar kinds of things can happen with embryos and foetuses. A cosmic ray passes through the embryo of one twin but not the other, causing mutation to a portion of DNA. One foetus lies closer to mum's reassuring heartbeat than the other. One gets flooded with just a little bit more hormone than the other. And so on.

Chance isn't something scientists are very comfortable with. On a cosmic level, maybe there's no such thing, but in terms of individual personality these random events could easily account for many of the differences between identical twins at birth. And they could equally account for some of the differences in personality between all of us.

What's the score?

So what were the factors responsible for making your personality 'special'? Here's how I see it in broad terms:

Genes	50%
The shared environment	15%
The unique environment	15%
The foetal environment	10%
Chance	10%

I'm sticking my neck out on some of this but there's very great agreement that genes account for around half of personality differences and that the shared environment accounts for relatively little (maybe even nothing at all, as we've seen). But that doesn't mean that as a parent you have no influence on anything to do with your children. You can certainly influence their behaviour, you can certainly introduce them to enough things for them to discover their aptitudes, and you can certainly support them in their struggles. And if, like Mr Polgár, you want to dedicate your life to the task, you probably have a very good chance of moulding your children to be what you want. But that's a very extreme case.

Self-coaching tip

Given that genes and other factors outside your control are responsible for so much, and upbringing relatively little, you can relax a bit as a parent. Your infant may not exhibit the personality you wanted but, rather than give both yourself and your child a hard time, you might as well be philosophical about it. Once you start accepting your child as an equal human being, rather than as a sort of experiment, you'll probably both be a lot happier.

10 TIPS FOR SUCCESS

1 No one is born a blank slate.

2 Some identical twins separated at birth develop uncannily similar personalities.

3 Genes are responsible for about half the differences in personality.

4 Genes are known to impact all the Big Five personality traits.

5 Genes can survive unchanged for millions of years – your personality may be quite 'primitive'.

6 Parenting (the 'shared environment') does not seem to have much impact on personality variation.

7 Group Socialization (who children play with) could be more important for personality than parental influence.

8 There's evidence for foetal memory as early as 22 weeks.

9 Some personality traits may be down to events in the womb.

10 Some personality traits may be down to chance.

11

The hidden self

In this chapter you will learn:
* *how your unconscious mind is really in control*
* *why you need to let chance enter your life*
* *how to play dice.*

True personality

John came from a 'good' family. His father had reached a fairly
eminent position in the legal profession and, as a consequence,
in the local community too. John was sent to boarding school.
Afterwards he had a 'wild' and 'rebellious' period. No one thought
too much of it. They saw it as just a 'phase he was going through'.
He let his hair grow and, being a fairly talented musician, joined
a band. But he was all too aware of what his family and friends
expected of him. Fairly soon he settled down to a job with a major
corporation, became a pillar of the local church, married a woman
whose ambitions included high social status, and had two children
who, in turn, he sent to public schools. His company's occasional
psychometric tests appeared to confirm he was in the right job.
But in his forties John's alcohol consumption got out of hand
and he had a breakdown. His life had been a lie and he could no
longer sustain it. He was trying to live up to something that, at
heart, he wasn't. John was torn between living up to other people's
expectations and living according to his true personality.

He obviously had the ability to do his job. His achievements
confirmed that. But, deep down, he didn't have the desire. His
conscious mind said one thing but his unconscious said another.

The invisible you

It's extraordinary and rather intriguing to realize that there is an invisible you. In fact, there are two. One is the you that is invisible to others but which you know very well. The other is the you that is invisible even to yourself. Just stop and think about it for a moment. Part of your mind is not under your direct control. You don't know what it's doing, or thinking right now and you certainly don't know what it's going to think or do in the future.

Suppose that you sometimes heard strange noises in your house. Supposing things happened that you couldn't quite account for. Then one day you discovered a door you'd never noticed before. Suppose you opened it and discovered to your astonishment that there were rooms you had never suspected and people whose existence you had never known. Having an unconscious mind is a bit like that, except that it's a lot harder to open the door.

Although you may not be aware of it, your unconscious mind plays an enormous role in your life. It runs your body, it stores your memories, it's responsible for your intuitions, it makes you do things you sometimes can't account for, and it reacts hundredths of a second faster than your conscious mind.

So let's take a look at some of the things the unconscious mind controls:

- ▶ memories that are easily available (some psychologists use the word 'pre-conscious' for this)
- ▶ distant memories
- ▶ repressed memories (made famous by Sigmund Freud)
- ▶ intuition
- ▶ dreams
- ▶ movement
- ▶ fast reactions
- ▶ bodily functions
- ▶ certain thoughts, attitudes and prejudices
- ▶ the collective unconscious (made famous by Carl Jung).

For the moment we just don't know the full extent of unconscious activity because, as yet, there's no objective way of scientifically measuring it as distinct from conscious activity. Various ingenious methods have been tried without much success, including the Rorschach test (see Chapter 4) and dream interpretation.

The power of dreams

In 1909 Carl Jung had a strange dream. In the dream he was on the top floor of an old house where he saw fine furnishings and paintings. He went down to the lower level and found a dark, medieval ambience. The floor was of stone slabs and in one of them was a ring. Lifting the slab he saw steps leading down into a cave and there he found bones, broken pottery and two human skulls. Then he awoke.

It's now probably the most famous dream in the world because Jung interpreted it as a model of the human psyche. The upper floor, according to Jung, represented the conscious personality and the ground floor represented the personal unconscious. But it was the cave that provided one of Jung's greatest contributions to the theory of the mind. As he saw it, the cave represented the *collective* unconscious, essentially the psychic heritage of all mankind.

As Jung saw it, his own unconscious had provided him with the insight that all human beings are born with certain common 'structures' inbuilt in their minds, which allow them to make sense of and relate to the world around them.

At the time, this seemed rather far-fetched but now that we know about genes (see the previous chapter) it doesn't seem far-fetched at all. The physical body has its pre-determined structures, which are roughly identical for all human beings all over the world. So why not the mind?

For most of us the relationship between a child and its mother is so commonplace and normal as to require no explanation. But Jung *did* require an explanation. If the psyche of a newborn baby is blank, then how does it know how to relate to a mother? Jung reasoned that the newborn mind already contained *archetypes* which he defined as 'identical psychic structures common to all'. The mother figure is an archetype. And there are many others.

Jung, like Freud, was a big believer in the significance of dreams. When the two men were together day after day on the steamer

George Washington from Bremen to New York, they analysed one another's. Freud believed that dreams were the 'royal road' to uncovering the unconscious and that they represented unfulfilled wishes. Perhaps that's why, in his own case, Freud was only willing to go so far. When Jung asked about certain details of Freud's private life, so as to be able to understand a dream better, Freud refused, saying, 'But I cannot risk my authority.'

It was a turning point in the relationship between Jung and the older and more famous Freud. 'That sentence,' wrote Jung, 'burned itself into my memory; and in it the end of our relationship was already foreshadowed. Freud was placing personal authority above truth.'

Of course, it may also simply have been that the father of psychoanalysis was himself embarrassed and inhibited. And perhaps unnecessarily, because many psychologists believe Freud was wrong in thinking that dreams represent unfulfilled wishes. We still know very little about them.

The simple facts are that we have an average of four dreaming periods a night, each lasting around 20 minutes and the majority, about 80 per cent, are unpleasant. We don't remember dreams much or at all unless we're waking up – because it's morning, because something has disturbed us, or because the dream itself has frightened us. That's a lot of dreaming, most of it not consciously recalled. But sometimes events in the real world correspond in some way with an earlier dream, triggering its memory. That's why some people come to believe their dream was actually a prophecy. Once again, it comes down to a misunderstanding of statistics and the probability of coincidences (see Chapter 6). By the same mechanism, dreams can seem to carry a message from the unconscious, as in the case of Jung's house and the cave underneath.

Other theories of dreams are that they're a sort of dress rehearsal for unpleasant things in life; that they're a way of (to use a computer analogy) defragmenting the hard drive of the mind, deleting unnecessary data and making new connections between useful data (thus occasionally coming up with solutions to problems that had been elusive in the daytime); and that they're utterly meaningless, being the products of random brain activity.

If your unconscious wants to communicate with your conscious, why would it use dream symbols rather than words? It makes the whole theory sound a little suspicious. Like spirits from the 'other side' who can only communicate with their relatives via a medium and never directly. But, in fact, there could be a perfectly logical explanation. The unconscious mind existed before words were invented and therefore had to develop a different kind of language. We can see something similar in the right hemisphere of the brain. It's the left hemisphere (in most people) that handles language (see Chapter 7). The right hemisphere just isn't as good with words.

Self-coaching tip

Even Freud, it seems, could be guilty of conformity. He was afraid to reveal things about himself to Jung that might have made him seem weird or not worthy of his position. The result was the opposite – Jung lost respect for him. You may remember from Chapter 8 how American psychologist Solomon Asch found that around 75 per cent of people would agree with the majority, even when their own senses told them something different. Interestingly, if just one person gave the correct lead, the level of conformity among the others fell dramatically to just 20 per cent. Be the one who breaks ranks and takes the lead.

Free will

In the 1930s, an American physician called Edmund Jacobson attached muscle sensors to volunteers and asked them to imagine various activities. He discovered that merely thinking about something caused an appropriate but tiny muscular response. In other words, if the volunteers were asked to imagine lifting a heavy weight, Jacobson's sensors picked up increased activity in the biceps.

So far, so logical. Probably, the ideomotor response, as it's known, is simply a mechanism that prepares the body for action. But things get more complicated. In the 1990s an American psychologist called Dan Wegner discovered that asking people *not* to do something also created the same kind of ideomotor response as if they had been asked to do it.

This is the explanation of all those spirit-driven moving tables, Ouija boards and swinging pendulums. When Wegner asked his volunteers to try very hard not to move a pendulum, they actually moved it more than those who had been asked simply to keep it still. This is known as the rebound effect and it operates at the unconscious level. Which is exactly why spiritualists and the like insist that they're not deliberately moving the tables or whatever. They, themselves, are not consciously aware of what they're doing.

But we're not finished yet. Things get more interesting still. Various researchers, including the neurophysiologist William Grey Walter and the physiologist Benjamin Libet, have conducted experiments which prove that the brain takes the decision to do something about a third of a second *before* you're consciously aware of it. Dan Wegner's explanation is that having taken the decision, your brain then sends out two sets of signals. One goes to the part of your brain that creates the conscious decision-making experience, and the other goes to the appropriate muscles, arriving a fraction of a second later.

If Wegner is right, the belief in a conscious decision-making process is simply an illusion. But if that's correct, where *is* the decision made? It can only be in the unconscious.

Ah, yes, you say, but the information that's contained in my unconscious is the result of my conscious decisions (to read a certain book, to study a particular subject at university, to live with a certain person, and so on). So, really, those unconscious decisions are actually conscious decisions.

But think again. That decision to go to university was only *apparently* a conscious decision. If the theory is right, the decision had already been taken by your unconscious mind. In fact, there was no *conscious* decision. What you took to be a conscious decision was, in fact, your unconscious *informing* your conscious of a decision that *it* (your unconscious) had already taken.

And the same goes for every 'conscious decision' you ever took, going back and back to the very first. That first decision was unconscious, not conscious.

For many things, this isn't so hard to accept. When you eat, for example, most of the necessary decisions (what food to put on your fork next, how fast to raise the fork to your mouth, when to open your mouth, how much to chew the food) are entirely in the unconscious realm. So should we be astonished to learn that all our decisions are, in fact, in the hands of this aspect of our brains?

This doesn't prove you have no free will. After all, your unconscious is still you. But the whole area becomes very muddied.

Can scientists in other disciplines help? In 2006, mathematicians John H. Conway and Simon B. Kochen attempted to settle the matter with their Free Will Theorem in *Foundations of Physics*. Testing the theorem requires a deep understanding of quantum physics but its implication can be stated like this. If a scientist is free to measure the spin of a particle in a way not determined by prior conditions, then the spin of the particle is also not determined by prior conditions. That's still pretty tricky to understand, so try this simple version. If people have free will, then so do electrons; if electrons don't have free will, then neither do people.

Until we can interview electrons we'll probably never know.

Insight

Do we ourselves even know what we truly think? It seems we may not. Various experiments have shown that whenever we try to put what we think into words, whether we speak them or write them down, our feelings become changed in the process. We just can't articulate with sufficient accuracy. So we end up changing our feelings to match the vocabulary we have available.

Self-coaching tip

Spend a minute looking at someone close to you, probably your partner or a good friend. Try not to use words at this stage. Just see that person and experience the emotions that follow. Now switch to words and, in no more than three sentences, try to express what you feel without using any clichés. How did you get on? Keep practising.

Why do I feel like this?

Psychologist Jim Alcock was driving a friend from the airport when both began thinking of a college classmate. Eager to discover why, Alcock retraced the route and discovered what had triggered their memories at the same moment. The college classmate had distinguished himself by always carrying a pendulum pedometer and in the window of a shop there was a pendulum clock. He and his friend had both spotted it but only unconsciously.

This kind of thing is going on all the time. In experiments, people have been shown pictures of snakes so briefly they didn't have time to work out what they were looking at. When asked to describe what they saw, they couldn't give a clear answer. And yet sensors attached to their skin detected increasing levels of sweat. They had felt fear. Their conscious minds didn't know what was going on but their unconscious minds did.

All emotions can be, and often are, unconscious. How do you feel right now, for example? Happy? Sad? Irritable? Placid? Do you know why? Very often we're not especially aware of our moods and, when we do become aware, we can't work out what made us feel that way. It could be something as unlikely as a headline in a newspaper seen out of the corner of an eye, a fragment of music drifting from an open window, or, as in the case of Jim Alcock, a pendulum clock. If you like the thing you've unconsciously noted, then you'll feel happy. But if you didn't like that college classmate, you might feel irritable without knowing why.

Emotions can also be spread from unconscious to unconscious. You know how some people are energizing and others are draining? That's often down to signals that are picked up at the unconscious level, mostly to do with body language.

But why should *their* emotions have an effect on *our* emotions? One theory is that it's because we unconsciously mimic other people. That's to say we match and mirror their posture and their movements, including their facial movements. If someone smiles we tend to smile and the very act of smiling makes us feel happier. If someone grimaces, we grimace and that makes us feel bad. In experiments, people do, indeed, emulate the expressions on other faces – happy, sad, angry and so on – albeit often at a level so subtle that only electronic sensors detected it.

So it seems as if we, like driftwood at sea, are very much at the mercy of the elements (especially in view of the Stanford prison experiment in Chapter 8). We go where the wind blows and then convince ourselves that the beach we end up on is what we'd intended all along. We can't even control our own minds. Is there nothing we can do to discover our hidden selves?

Maybe there is.

The dice man and woman

In the 1960s, a university professor with a degree in psychology had the idea of letting his life be directed by throws of the dice. His name was George Cockcroft and his notion became *The Dice Man*, the cult novel of 1971, written under the pen name of Luke Rhinehart.

We're going to play the same game, but a little differently. Rhinehart's life wasn't entirely dictated by chance throws of the dice since he himself decided in advance what each number would require him to do. He was still controlling the options which, to make the novel more gripping, were usually dangerous, immoral or illegal. We're going to be both more adventurous and more cautious. More adventurous because you're not going to choose the options. I am. But also more cautious because nothing will be dangerous, immoral or illegal – just very, very revealing.

I want you to get two dice and throw them one at a time. The uppermost dots on the first die give your first digit. And the uppermost on the second die give your second digit. In other words, if you throw a three followed by a five, then the dice have chosen 35. The smallest number you can throw is, therefore, 11 and the largest is 66.

Having thrown the dice, refer to the list which follows this explanation and do as instructed. You may not necessarily be able to do the thing at once but you should *immediately* set the wheels in motion. A week later, repeat the procedure and follow the new instruction (still continuing the previous one if it's ongoing). Carry on in this way (but as your diary fills up you may have to throw the dice less frequently). Often, having had an experience, you'll decide it's not for you. That's okay. There's no need to carry on with it indefinitely, *but you must continue long enough to make a proper evaluation*. Then you can stop, if you want. The idea is simply to try things you might not otherwise have done. On the other hand, it may be you like it so much that you want to keep on doing it. That's also okay. Over time you could find your life filling up with all kinds of new interests, but always make space to keep trying new things.

Self-coaching tip

You could learn to do some of the things entirely from books but part of the idea is to come into contact with people who have ideas that are different from yours. That's very important. So try to learn from other people and with other people whenever you can. Certainly buy books (you'll find many useful titles in the Teach Yourself series) but, one way or another, get into contact with experts and enthusiasts. (There are, however, a few options that require a degree of solitude.)

Periodically, replenish the list with new experiences chosen *at random* from, say, directories, so you've always got plenty of options. If you have a partner, by all means involve him or her (sometimes that will be essential), and friends too, when appropriate. That can add enormously to the fun.

The most interesting results come about when you throw the dice and say, 'Oh no, not that!' The whole point, after all, is to experience things you wouldn't ever have chosen to do. If you throw the dice and say, 'Oh, goodee', then you're probably not going to learn anything new about yourself.

Remember, you *must* follow the decision of the dice. The only circumstances in which you can throw again are (a) that you've fully experienced the choice already and (b) that it genuinely is physically beyond you. If the selection is more or less impossible on account of the weather, you can defer it to another week but you can't annul it.

Insight

Some of the options are *potentially* expensive but you can usually find a cheaper solution. Rather than take a formal sailing course, for example, you can offer yourself as crew (look on the internet). Or as payment for riding lessons you could offer to do unpaid work at a stable. And sometimes there are clubs where members teach one another. In fact, tracking down enthusiasts and convincing them to help you can be as fascinating as actually gaining the skills themselves. I learned various things in this way (to a greater or lesser degree) including sailing, riding (and shoeing), playing flamenco guitar, diving, snowboarding, caving and French.

Here, then, from 11 to 66, are your options:

11 Ask someone who has a different belief system to your own (an atheist, Hindu, Christian, Buddhist, etc.) to teach you about it – working through a book together can be a good basis.

12 Take a course of riding lessons – at least six.

13 Go hiking for at least a weekend in the wildest place that's within a reasonable distance, camping out for at least one night.

14 Take at least six lessons on a musical instrument.

15 Take a course on Tantric sex or buy a book and follow the instructions (even if you don't have a partner at the moment there are still things you can learn and do).

16 Take swimming lessons, either as a beginner or as an improver.

21 Take a boating course of some kind (canoe, dinghy, yacht or whatever) for at least a weekend on a suitable lake or river or in the sea.

22 Be a vegan for one week (try to get advice from people who are vegans).

23 Switch roles for a day with your partner. You do everything your partner would have done and your partner does everything you would have done. Try to think and be like your partner. If you don't have a partner, swap roles with someone else.

24 Take a course in creative writing.

25 Go to a nudist beach and swim naked or, if there's no such place within a reasonable distance (and *only* then), spend a day naked at home.

26 Join any society that involves performing in public (debating, acting, singing, etc.) or take a course in clowning or to be a stand-up comedian.

31 Take a course in meditation, yoga or tai chi.

32 Go to a performance of any kind of music that you 'don't like' (pop, jazz, baroque, opera or whatever).

33 Take a climbing course, either outdoors or at a climbing wall.

34 Undertake some charity work such as volunteering for an environment improvement project, or to help in an animal refuge, or to assist the elderly.

35 Learn a foreign language and, as part of that, correspond with a pen friend in another country.

36 Spend an entire day on your own ambling in the countryside without speaking.

41 Take a course in painting, sculpture or photography.

42 Take dancing lessons.
43 If you have a partner, spend an entire day in bed together, listening to music, massaging one another, declaring your love and making love; if you don't have a partner, spend an entire day in bed pampering yourself in every possible way.
44 Read the manifesto of a political party you think you disagree with.
45 Learn a practical skill such as carpentry, brick laying or metal working.
46 Take a guided bird watching tour.
51 Learn skiing or snowboarding (at a snowdome or elsewhere), skateboarding, in-line skating, ice-skating or surfing.
52 Take a course in interior design and transform one room of your home.
53 Buy or borrow clothing completely different to your normal style and wear it for a day.
54 Spend time with someone whose sexuality is different to yours and compare notes on attraction, emotions and sexual tastes.
55 Go on a potholing weekend.
56 Try something to do with flying such as a flying lesson, parascending, gliding, or ballooning.
61 Investigate six completely different types of career.
62 Start a campaign for or against something in your local area or on the internet, or join a protest march
63 If you're in dating mode, try to go out with someone who's 'not your type'; if you're already happily in a relationship, strike up a friendship with someone who's 'not your type'.
64 Go to a restaurant and eat food you believe you won't like.
65 Tell your partner, best friend or closest relative six things about yourself that you've kept hidden, and ask that person to reveal six things to you.
66 Travel for 66 minutes in any direction, by any means of transport, and, having arrived, involve yourself in the lives of the people there.

Why have I asked you to do this? Well, the simple reason is that you can't know if you do or don't like something until you've had some sort of experience of it. You may assume you'll hate it but, when it comes to it, you may surprise yourself by loving it. Each experience has the potential to take you in a new direction and give you the opportunity to discover things about your personality that you'd never suspected.

10 TIPS FOR SUCCESS

1 Part of you is hidden from others; part of you is hidden even from yourself.

2 Your unconscious mind reacts hundredths of a second faster than your conscious mind and is responsible for a lot of your personality.

3 Jung believed that all human minds contain the same *archetypes* which he defined as 'identical psychic structures common to all'.

4 Freud believed dreams represented repressed desires, but it may be they're nothing more than junk.

5 Just thinking about doing something produces a tiny but appropriate muscular response.

6 Asking people not to make a movement results in them making that very movement.

7 It may be that it's your unconscious mind that always takes decisions – what you think of as a conscious decision is simply your unconscious *informing* you of the decision it's already taken.

8 We often change our emotions to fit the words available to us.

9 Things that we perceive unconsciously can have a significant impact on our emotions.

10 Deliberately letting chance enter your life is one way of letting your unconscious find the right path.

12

Tackling high Neuroticism

In this chapter you will learn:
- *that aspects of personalitsy can be changed or modulated*
- *the importance of controlling your conscious thoughts*
- *cognitive therapy (CT).*

You're about to embark on the most exhilarating section of this book. In the past few days you've discovered a huge amount about your personality, and that's already been a tremendously exciting journey. But you're now on the brink of something truly awesome. We're about to investigate the possibility that you can actually *change* your personality; that you can modify some of the very things you've just discovered about yourself.

Let's just remind ourselves what it is you'd be doing if you succeeded. You'd be modifying something about your habitual pattern of thoughts, feelings and behaviour. To make it meaningful, I think you'd have to score higher or lower than you do now in one of the Big Five traits. And that new score would have to be permanent, so that you almost always display this new style.

Do we have any hope? We certainly do.

I'm assuming that if you want to make any change to your score for Neuroticism that you'll want to make it lower. That's what this chapter is about. In the next chapter, I'll be looking at ways of giving you a higher score for the other Big Five traits of Openness, Conscientiousness, Extroversion and Agreeableness. However, should you wish to achieve the opposite for any trait, the techniques can be adapted.

The 'ecology check'

But, first of all, is there anything you *really* want to change? Think very carefully about this. If it's not something you feel deep down, none of the techniques in this chapter or the next will achieve very much. You seriously have to want to change.

You also need to ponder the impact on the people around you. Would they want you to change in the way you have in mind? Will it make life better for them, or worse?

These are big questions. In Neuro-Linguistic Programming (NLP), a family of techniques I'll be describing later, it's normal to carry out what's known as an 'ecology check'.

The key questions are:

- ▶ What will happen if I succeed in making this change?
- ▶ What won't happen if I succeed in making this change?
- ▶ What will happen if I don't succeed in making this change?
- ▶ What won't happen if I don't succeed in making this change?

I suggest you consider these four questions very carefully before employing any of the techniques described in this chapter and the next.

Self-coaching tip

Nothing in this chapter is magic. It all requires a certain amount of effort. You won't make any permanent changes by utilizing the techniques once only. You have to keep practising until new responses become automatic. Only then can you say you've genuinely changed something in your personality.

Cognitive therapy

The principle of cognitive therapy (CT) is that the way you feel is governed by the way you think. Or to put it another way, thoughts precede emotions.

If you generally feel low, putting on a funny film may or may not bring you some relief. But if it does it will only be temporary. That's because you're trying to come at things via your emotions. To achieve something more permanent – to change your personality – you need to tackle your thinking, and to change it irrevocably. It will take time, but it can be done.

Using CT we'll be trying to change the following ten kinds of thinking that are associated with high Neuroticism:

1 Comparing with others (Example: Theirs is better.)
2 Materialism (Example: I don't have enough.)
3 All-or-nothingism (Example: If I'm not rich, I'm a failure.)
4 Perfectionism (Example: If it's not perfect, it's no good.)
5 Exaggerating the negative (Example: Why is this always happening to me?)
6 Jumping to negative conclusions (Example: I'm not going to like this.)
7 Emotional reasoning (Example: I feel bad, so it must be bad.)
8 Labelling (Example: I'm a failure; you're a success.)
9 Feeling of obligation (Example: I should do this.)
10 Wrongly taking responsibility (Example: If it's wrong it must be my fault.)

Now let's take a look at these ways of thinking in detail.

COMPARING WITH OTHERS

If you're always comparing yourself with the most fortunate people on the planet (at least, as you see them), then you're bound to undermine your self-esteem and make yourself miserable.

Let me ask you this. Are you happier when you listen to music on an MP3 player than when you listen to the same music on a CD player? And did the music on the CD player make you happier than listening to it on a tape cassette? And did the cassette make you happier than listening to an old-fashioned LP? Of course not. It's the music that counts. You don't have to have the latest or the most expensive gadget in order to enjoy life.

Insight

Advertising is, in some ways, one of the greatest curses of our era because it forces us to compare ourselves with the richest, most beautiful and (apparently) happiest people on the planet. Ignore it.

MATERIALISM

If you're the kind of person who always has to have more and more, then, by definition, you'll never be happy. Even for Bill Gates there has to be a limit.

Does money buy happiness? Well, as we saw in Chapter 9, there's no doubt that an inability to pay the bills causes unhappiness. And there's no doubt, either, that having insufficient disposable income for a few of life's little pleasures causes unhappiness.

So money can certainly 'cure' some of the causes of unhappiness. But that's not the same thing at all as saying that money creates happiness. In fact, there's very little evidence for a strong positive effect of wealth on happiness. A person who earns half a million a year isn't 20 times happier than a person earning 25,000, nor even twice as happy – maybe, at a pinch, 10 per cent happier; maybe not at all.

Several studies have shown that when people win large sums of money, they don't become happier in the medium to longer term. Nor are people generally happier in wealthier countries compared with poorer countries. Nor does increase in national wealth result in more happiness. Americans seem to be no happier now than they were in 1946/7 and considerably less happy than they were in the late 1950s.

So while poverty causes misery, we can dispense with wealth as a significant cause of happiness.

Insight

The bottom line is this: most of us are never going to be very wealthy, so the debate is academic. If you're not rich, you still want to be happy. And you can be, if you have the right attitude. You're better to spend money on experiences rather than things, because the memories remain long after the things have worn out.

Self-coaching tips

1 Start a 'happiness diary'. After a month, review it to see where most of your happiness has been coming from. Is it from material possessions or life's inexpensive pleasures?
2 This month, don't buy anything other than necessities and don't use any expensive products (except where you have no alternative). Concentrate on finding happiness in things that are free or inexpensive, such as love, sex, friendship, pets, nature, swimming in the sea or a lake, walking or running, and identifying the stars.
3 If you do spend money, direct it at enjoyable experiences rather than material goods.

ALL-OR-NOTHINGISM

This is a style of thinking that keeps life simple but it makes no allowance for reality, which is that between black and white there are infinite shades of grey. Most of the time the black and white mentality leads to a good deal of misery. Either you're a success or you're a failure. Either you're attractive or you're ugly. Either you're a great raconteur or you're a bore. And since nobody is in the top drawer in every category, anyone with this outlook is going to feel despondent a lot of the time.

PERFECTIONISM

If you're meticulous and painstaking, then you score high for Conscientiousness. But the degree of perfectionism we're concerned with here is something different and comes under the heading of high Neuroticism. It's striving for a level so unrealistically extreme that you're either so intimidated you can't even begin or you're reluctant ever to pronounce something 'finished'. However commendable the attitude, it has no practical use. You just end up making yourself unhappy along with everybody else you're involved with.

You may believe, as so many do, that perfection does exist. But I'm going to prove to you that in terms of the things human beings do, it doesn't. Oh, OK, if I ask you two plus two and you answer four, then, yes, that's the perfect answer. But let's look at things that are a little more complicated.

The test is this. If something is perfect, it's incapable of improvement. So let's take a look around. Let's take your TV. Is the picture quality so good it could never be improved? Obviously not. Could your car be more durable, quieter, more fuel efficient? Obviously it could. Have you ever seen a film in which every line of dialogue was convincing, every gesture accurate, every camera angle satisfying and the plot always clear? No. I won't go on. When you think about it you'll see that perfection of that kind doesn't exist.

Obviously you have ideals of some sort. And it's important that you do. But, very often, ideals also involve a concept of perfection that's impossible to attain. Never give yourself a hard time because you fall short of those kinds of ideals. (And don't give anybody else a hard time either because they fall short of your ideals.) Rather, congratulate yourself when you move closer to your ideals. Or, better still, set yourself ideals that are more realistic.

Insight

If you think you've been delivering perfection up till now, then I've got news for you – you're mistaken. But, of course, you didn't really think that, did you! No human being ever delivers perfection. But by striving for perfection and thinking you must achieve perfection, you're creating a barrier. In my profession we call it 'writers' block'. It's when you're so anxious to create a masterpiece that you can't actually function at all. Believe me, the people who pay you are going to be far happier if you produce three pieces of competent work rather than one piece of 'perfect' work.

Self-coaching tip

Whatever you have to do today, set out to do it to a good and competent standard, but not to perfection. At the end of the day work out how much you got through compared with a perfectionist day.

EXAGGERATING THE NEGATIVE

Most of us focus far too much on the negative and, what's more, exaggerate the significance of anything that goes wrong. The whole thing is summed up in that well-known phrase: Why is this always happening to me?

You know the kind of thing. You get a bird-dropping on your clothes and you say it. You get a puncture and you say it. You get a parking ticket and you say it. And yet it's never true. You get a parking ticket once a year, a bird dropping on your clothes once in five years and a puncture once a decade.

Insight

What makes you notice the bad things is not that they always happen but that they happen *so seldom*. In fact, if they always happened you wouldn't bother to mention the subject.

Self-coaching tips

Instead of focusing on the negative, try focusing on the positive for a change. Let's start with you. What are your good points? I want you to write them down. You don't have to be 'world class' in any of them to add them to your list. Here are some suggestions to get you going:

▶ I don't deliberately harm anybody else.
▶ I always make time for my friends when they have problems.
▶ I'm quite good at telling jokes and making people laugh.
▶ I don't make a fuss when things go wrong.
▶ I'm good at drawing.
▶ Dogs like me.

Now you make your own list.

If you really can't think of anything, then you're being too hard on yourself. In fact, if your sheet of paper is blank or with only a couple of points written down, then we don't have to look very far for one of the sources of your unhappiness. You don't like yourself enough. You don't love yourself enough. Well, you should. For a start, you're certainly modest. So put that down. You're obviously sensitive. So put that down. You're also introspective. Add that to the list. That's three useful qualities already.

Many unhappy people simply demand too much of themselves and those around them, too. We're all human beings – animals, in fact – with enormous limitations. You're going to have to learn to accept that about yourself and your fellow man and woman. Just do your best. Nobody can ask more. Now get back to the list and don't stop until you've got at least 20 things written down.

When you've finished writing about yourself, make a list of all the good points about your partner. Again, here are some suggestions to get you going:

- ▶ He/she seldom gets angry.
- ▶ He/she never spends money without discussing it with me first.
- ▶ He/she is always very considerate towards my parents.
- ▶ He/she looks after me when I'm ill.
- ▶ He/she likes many of the same things I do.
- ▶ He/she makes me laugh.
- ▶ He/she cooks beautiful meals for me.

And then do the same for your children, your parents and anyone else you're close to.

Next you're going to make a list of all the good things in your life. For example:

- ▶ I'm in good health.
- ▶ I have somewhere nice to live.
- ▶ I never have to go hungry.
- ▶ I have many friends.

Begin with your body. If it works pretty much as it should, then that's already something to be very happy about. Can you see? Can you hear? Can you touch things? Can you taste things? Can you smell them? Can you remember things? Can you run? Can you swim? Can you make love? This is going to be a pretty long list.

Nobody's list should – could – be short. If yours is, then you've got to learn to appreciate things more than you do. You're taking far too much for granted. You've got to learn to stop comparing with the ultimate – the richest person, the biggest house, the strongest athlete, the most beautiful face – and try to get a bit more perspective. Don't forget there are also people who have almost nothing to eat, who don't have any kind of house and who combat severe disabilities.

When you've finished your lists, copy them out very clearly onto some card or, if you have a computer, print them. Also make the 'highlights' into a portable version you can keep in your wallet or handbag. Make sure you always have copies close to hand. Here's what you do.

- ▶ When you get up in the morning, read the lists.
- ▶ When you're having lunch, read the lists.

▶ Just before you go to sleep, read the lists.
▶ Any time you're feeling unhappy or cross with your partner or people close to you, read the lists.

Insight

It probably sounds a rather silly idea to make lists of positive things, but it's been proven to work in many experiments. In fact, it's an extremely powerful technique for overcoming the negative thinking associated with high Neuroticism. So *do* try it. And not just for a day. It's going to take your brain some time to rewire itself with this new and more positive way of looking at the world. Try it for at least a month.

JUMPING TO NEGATIVE CONCLUSIONS

Your partner is late. You look at your watch and begin to get angry. A little while later your anger starts to become overlaid by concern. 'He's had an accident.' 'She's been abducted.' You're worried and very unhappy.

After an hour your partner arrives. What happened? It turns out to have been nothing more than a simple misunderstanding over the time. One of you thought you'd agreed on 8 o'clock, the other 9 o'clock.

These kinds of situations happen: the people whispering in the corner, who – you convince yourself – are saying bad things about you; the boss who doesn't greet you in the usual, cheerful way because – you convince yourself – he's about to reprimand you; the medical test, which – you convince yourself – is bound to have found a life-threatening condition.

Insight

We all like to have a go at predicting the future and enjoy saying 'I told you so' when our forecasts turn out to be right. And the predictions are usually negative. But we tend to forget the occasions when we were wrong.

Self-coaching tips

Let's find out how often you're justified in jumping to negative conclusions. Carry a notebook with you for the next week. Every time a negative prediction comes into your mind, write it down. Things like:

▶ I'm never going to be able to do this.
▶ He's going to cause trouble for me.

- She isn't going to like me.
- They look very suspicious.
- There's no way out of this.
- It can only mean something terrible has happened.

When the outcome of the situation is known, write it in your notebook. At the end of the week, tot up how many times your negative predictions turned out to be right and how many wrong. You'll almost certainly find the latter outweigh the former by a considerable margin. That's an awful lot of anxiety over nothing. Now try writing down positive predictions and see how many times they come true. Yes, more often than you think!

Insight

You may feel that you need to anticipate the worst so you can be ready to defend yourself against it. But in reality you're wasting a lot of energy and making yourself unhappy quite needlessly. Look at it this way. What have you got to lose by adopting a positive stance? 'The people in the corner are discussing their sex lives.' 'The boss is preoccupied.' 'The results of my medical test will be fine.' Of course, there are occasions when it would be prudent to take some action, but you can still do that without having to visualize worst-case scenarios. Believe the best until you have reason to know otherwise.

EMOTIONAL REASONING

The ugly duckling who becomes a swan is a story that goes back as long as stories have been told. The duckling feels ugly (usually because of things others have said) and comes to believe it must be true. And so it can be with many other emotions. You feel like a failure and conclude that you are a failure. You feel nobody likes you and conclude that you're unlovable. You feel you can't cope and conclude you're a bad mother. But your feelings can be wrong. For sure, you're far more of a swan than you realize.

Self-coaching tip

Next time you feel the kinds of emotions that undermine your self-esteem, write them down. Then try to analyse the situation objectively. If you can't, enlist the help of a friend. Write down six reasons why your emotion wasn't justified.

LABELLING

As with the black and white approach, labels can make life simpler. I'm a loser. He's an idiot. She's stupid. They're unbeatable. Once the label has been decided, there's no need to look any more deeply or keep the situation under review. And that's exactly why labelling is a disaster. It's far too simplistic, takes no account of change and, worst of all, is self-fulfilling.

For example, when you go to play the tennis partners who are 'unbeatable', you'll have given up before even hitting the first ball. When you decide you're a 'loser', you won't even try any more. And when you treat other people as 'idiots', you don't give them the opportunity to tackle problems and grow.

Self-coaching tips

1 Write down the names of all the people to whom you've attributed labels. Include yourself, if you've given yourself a label. Next to the names write the label. Now, in each case find six reasons why the label is inappropriate.

2 Choose a subject at which you've labelled yourself a failure and given up trying (I can't dance/play tennis/do maths, or whatever). Then take lessons from a properly qualified teacher. You may not be the best but you'll discover that you're certainly not a 'failure' either.

FEELING OF OBLIGATION

We all have a little voice within telling us what we should do. (And quite often it's reinforced by someone else's voice, too.) I should cut the grass, even though it's only an inch long. I should clean the house, even though I did it last week. I should go to Bill and Sheila's party, even though we have nothing in common. And when you don't do what you should, you feel guilt. Guilt is a very unpleasant emotion to have to deal with.

Maybe you also direct 'should statements' at others. You should smarten yourself up a bit. You should go to the funeral. You should get a better job. If the people you're directing the statements at don't take any notice, you end up feeling frustrated and resentful.

> ### Self-coaching tips
>
> 1 For the next week banish all 'shoulds' and see what happens. Each time you're faced with a 'should situation', apply a different mindset to it: Taking all things into account, will I be happier if I do this or if I don't?
> 2 As regards other people, ask yourself this: What right have I got to tell someone else what to do?

Insight
Sometimes there just are things you've got to do, whether you like it or not. In that case, you may as well do them with good grace and maximize whatever pleasure you can find. But those occasions are far fewer than you think. We're concerned with happiness not 'shoulds'.

WRONGLY TAKING RESPONSIBILITY

Accepting responsibility for things that aren't your responsibility is a common error, particularly among women. Women are the nurturing sex so it's understandable that they react this way more often than men do.

Let's say that your elderly father insists on driving. He hasn't had an accident yet but you're convinced it's only a matter of time – and not very much time. You feel it's your responsibility to tell him to sell the car. You lie awake at night worrying about how to persuade him – and how he'll manage without it. You're unhappy.

But let's look at the facts. Your father is an adult, with more experience than you have, and makes his own decisions. He hasn't had an accident, which probably means he's acknowledged his limitations and drives accordingly. The police haven't interfered. His doctor hasn't interfered. So why should you?

Insight

When you love someone, it's only natural that you should want to intervene. But you're going to have to accept that there are things beyond your control and that other people have free will and ideas of their own. Quite possibly, you like the feeling that other people can't do without you and that you're indispensable. That's not a terrible thing as long as it's not taken to an extreme. The problem comes when you start to worry and make yourself unhappy over something that really isn't your responsibility.

Turning a negative inner voice into a constructive partner

Now we're going to try a completely different approach to the problem of high Neuroticism. Neuro-Linguistic Programming (NLP) is a whole family of techniques, originally developed by Richard Bandler and John Grinder, and expanded over the years by various contributors. NLP has a number of 'presuppositions' for living more constructively. The one we're interested in right now is:

▶ Underlying every behaviour is a positive intention.

In other words, when your inner voice is saying negative things about you, it's doing it for a good reason. You need to find out that reason. How? Simply by starting a conversation. Like this:

You: Why do you keep criticizing me?

Inner voice: Because I want you to sharpen up and pay attention to what you're doing.

You: Well, you're having completely the opposite effect because you're demoralizing me.

Inner voice: So you're weak on top of everything else! Can't take criticism!

You': I'm telling you, if you don't improve I'm getting rid of you.

Inner voice: You wish! Listen, you've got to stop making stupid mistakes.

You: So tell me how. Be more constructive.

Inner voice: All right. You need more patience. Be willing to spend a little more time on preparation before you rush into things. Then you'll be fine.

You: Why couldn't you have put it like that to begin with?

Did you find that conversation comical or even absurd? If so, you're going to find Six Step Reframing something of a revelation, because you'll be talking to your unconscious in just this way, as if it's a separate person. In this example, we're using it to change the negativity of your unconscious as regards – let's say – any potentially dangerous physical activity. If you're very anxious when confronted with physical challenges, then this will definitely help. At first Six Step Reframing may well strike you as a little wacky. However, once you try it, you'll fairly soon get used to the idea.

Step 1: Identify the behaviour to be changed – in this example, it's the negativity of your unconscious.

Step 2: Get your unconscious to communicate via a reliable involuntary signal. Grinder suggests asking something like: 'Will you, my unconscious, communicate with me?' You must then wait passively with your attention focused on your body for a signal from your unconscious. If you receive a signal, touch the area of your body where the signal occurred and say, 'Thank you'. To check, you then ask: 'If the signal just offered means yes, please repeat it.' You now need to validate the signal. Asking your unconscious to remain inactive, you now try to reproduce the signal consciously. If you can, then the possibility exists that the signal wasn't a genuine signal from the unconscious and you'll need to repeat the process until you have an authentic involuntary signal.

Step 3: Discover the positive intention behind the behaviour to be changed. In this case you could ask your unconscious: 'What is the positive intention behind the negative comments?' Let's assume you get the answer, 'To prevent you doing something in which you might get hurt.'

Step 4: Having discovered the positive intention, you now need to generate a set of alternatives as good or better than the original behaviour at satisfying that positive intention. Ask your unconscious: 'Develop an alternative range of behaviours all of which satisfy the positive intention while nevertheless helping me achieve my goal and from those select up to three for implementation. When you have completed the task give me a positive signal.'

Step 5: The alternative behaviours should now be apparent to you. For example, your unconscious might agree to drop the negative comments if you (a) accept the need to take more lessons, (b) agree to practise the basic manoeuvres more thoroughly, (c) be willing to wear protective clothing. Get your unconscious to accept responsibility for implementing the new behaviours. For example, you might ask: 'Will you, my unconscious mind, take responsibility for making sure the new behaviours are followed?'

Step 6: Carry out an ecology check (see the start of this chapter) by asking the unconscious to make sure that none of the new behaviours will cause a problem for you or for others.

Insight

Examples of the kind of signal your unconscious could give you that you couldn't very easily reproduce consciously (Step 2) include: tingling down the back of your neck or spine, fluttering or pulsating of a muscle, a localized hot or tickling sensation, a localized numbness.

10 TIPS FOR SUCCESS

1 Your personality can be described as your habitual pattern of thoughts, feelings and behaviour.

2 It is possible to make changes to your personality.

3 The proof of a genuine personality change would be a permanently higher or lower score in one of the Big Five traits.

4 Before attempting to change your personality, you should carry out an 'ecology check'.

5 All techniques for personality change need to be practised regularly.

6 The principle of cognitive therapy (CT) is that the way you feel is governed by the way you think.

7 To reduce high Neuroticism there are ten negative ways of thinking that may need to be tackled.

8 Neuro-Linguistic Programming (NLP) is a whole family of techniques, originated by Richard Bandler and John Grinder.

9 Underlying every behaviour is a positive intention.

10 Six Step Reframing is an effective technique for persuading your inner voice to be more constructive.

13

Increasing your personality scores

In this chapter you will learn:
- *how you can become whatever you visualize*
- *how to be a movie star*
- *how to hypnotize yourself.*

In the last chapter, we looked at ways of reducing your score for Neuroticism. In this chapter we'll be seeing how you can increase your scores for the remaining Big Five traits of Openness, Conscientiousness, Extroversion and Agreeableness, using visualization techniques adapted from the Neuro-Linguistic Programming (NLP) family. We'll also be using the very powerful technique of self-hypnosis.

Visualization

Visualization has been taken to a whole new level by NLP founders John Grinder and Richard Bandler. You probably already use visualization but more in the realm of fantasy, murdering someone who has annoyed you or having sex with someone you're attracted to. What's different about NLP visualization is that Bandler and Grinder looked to the techniques of the cinema and copied them. The result is something very focused and very powerful. Here are some of the possible techniques:

▶ multiple camera positions
▶ zooming in and out

- ▶ dialogue
- ▶ music
- ▶ voiceover
- ▶ multiple screens
- ▶ sound effects
- ▶ slow-motion
- ▶ freeze frame
- ▶ stills
- ▶ changing from colour to black-and-white or sepia tinting
- ▶ soft focus.

Have a bit of fun with these ideas. Lie back right now, close your eyes, conjure up a scene and begin exploring it like a film director. Move your 'camera' around to see things from different angles – from in front, behind, underneath, looking down from the ceiling or from a helicopter. Experiment with dialogue, voiceover, music and sound effects, and throw in a few tricks such as soft focus and slow-motion. You're limited only by your imagination. There are no budgetary or physical constraints.

Enjoy yourself but at the same time take note of the psychological impact of the different techniques and particularly of the qualities of images, sounds and textures. In NLP, these kinds of qualities are known as 'submodalities' and by manipulating them you can change the way you feel about things. For example, if you're low in Extroversion, you possibly tend towards muted colours when you visualize a group of people. By switching to bright colours (and, perhaps, loud, exuberant music) you'll respond more as someone high in Extroversion would.

YOUR FIRST EXERCISE

In this example we're going to try to increase your scores for Extroversion and Agreeableness, but you can equally use it for working on any of the Big Five. What you're going to do is conjure up a group of people towards whom you'd like to direct those qualities and imagine yourself behaving in that way. Really try to see and hear yourself and enjoy the way the other people respond to you.

1 Use different camera positions. Sometimes the camera is on you, sometimes on the other people, and sometimes at a distance showing all of you.

2 Make the colours more vivid.

3 Add dialogue. Hear yourself speaking. Hear the other people laughing at your jokes.

4 Make your voice sound more confident and relaxed.

5 Add some party music.

6 Build the music up to a crescendo.

7 Add a voiceover. Hear the commentator saying what an enjoyable companion you are.

8 Use multiple screens. Visualize, say, half the screen taken up by your face. The other half is split into a dozen compartments, each with the face of someone enjoying your conversational skills.

9 Increase the way your skin shines and intensify the sparkle in your eyes until it's dazzling.

10 Employ slow-motion and soft focus as you lead the group away, all of them eager to enjoy some exciting experience together with you.

Insight

Don't worry if you can't visualize things very clearly. Very few people can. Usually it's a question of seeing a scene, or a fragment of a scene, for just a moment. But that's enough to get started. The more you practise, the better you'll get at it and the more powerful the impact will be.

THE MAGIC CIRCLE

NLP has a visualization technique known as the Circle of Confidence. Some people climb mountains or sail round the world single-handed to try to convince themselves that they can have the self-confidence to tackle just about any situation. They theorize that if they take on the world's hardest challenges, then nothing else will ever seem difficult again. NLP does things differently. It lets you take the self-confidence you felt in any previous situation, including one that was *easy*. And then it transfers that feeling to the more difficult situation.

However, the technique can be adapted for any of the Big Five, which is why I prefer to call it The Magic Circle. In this example I'm going to use it to increase Openness.

Step 1: Something important is coming up that will require you to be extremely creative, finding a solution that demonstrates flair and imagination.

Step 2: Search your memory for a past occasion when you felt your creative juices flowing. It doesn't have to have been an especially difficult challenge. It can even have been when you were a child before you were, perhaps, made to conform. Relive that creative time, seeing and hearing everything in as much detail as possible. Particularly notice how you looked and how confidence in your creative powers was oozing out of you.

Step 3: Imagine a circle on the floor. Take the creative charge you feel and pour it into the circle. Immediately the circle takes on a colour – the colour that, to you, is the colour of creativity. It also makes a noise. Maybe it's a buzzing sound or even music – again, it's whatever expresses creativity to you.

Step 4: Are there any other qualities you'll need? Maybe a touch of iconoclasm? Maybe a dash of mysticism? If so, repeat the procedure, also pouring those qualities into your circle.

Step 5: Turn your thoughts to the future occasion when you'll be wanting to feel those qualities. Select a cue to that moment. For example, if you're going to a brainstorming session, the cue could be a secretary calling your name. (But don't make it too specific otherwise you might never get the cue you envisaged.)

Step 6: Holding that cue in your mind, step into the circle and visualize all those qualities rising up from the floor, permeating and enveloping you. As you move around, so that cocoon of creativity will move with you.

Step 7: Visualize the future unfolding from that cue moment. See yourself behaving with creativity and all the other qualities you've selected.

Step 8: When the cue moment arrives for real, visualize the circle on the floor, step into it and go and do what you have to do.

SWISHING

Swishing is a way of creating an emotion with one image and then quickly substituting a new image which, as a result, acquires the same emotional charge as the first. Here we're going to use it for impulse control (high Conscientiousness), but again you can use it for other things. And, of course, you can use it together with The Magic

Circle. The more techniques you have at your disposal and the more frequently you use them, the more powerful the effect.

Find yourself somewhere comfortable and quiet. Propping yourself up on your bed is ideal. If you prefer, you can practise Steps 1, 3 and 4 on separate occasions. Once you're proficient at them, you can put the whole procedure together and run through it in its entirety, from beginning to end, the necessary number of times.

Step 1: Your first task is to think of the kind of situation in which you need to have more impulse control. A situation in which you have felt unable to control yourself in the past and which you know is going to occur again in the future. When it does, you don't want to feel inadequate any more. You want to feel that you will acquit yourself well in your own eyes and in the eyes of other people. Really enter into that unsatisfactory experience. See, hear, smell, taste and touch as much of it as possible. If anybody is saying anything, or you're saying anything, whether out loud or in your head, take note of it. Also note where in your body you experience the feeling that the temptation is too great. In your stomach, perhaps? Take your time over this. This is the cue image.

Step 2: Clear the screen. This is a little bit like eating a small piece of bread before going on to taste the next wine. The idea is simply to wipe the images from Step 1 so that your mind is ready for the next visualization. If you find it difficult to clear your head, try reciting your telephone number backwards.

Step 3: Now you're going to build an image of yourself the way you'd *like* to be. The way you'd look and feel if you had complete mastery of the cue image situation and *had already successfully dealt with it.* This is the 'you' that, in fact, you're going to become very shortly. We'll call this version 'wonderful you'. Spend plenty of time building the image of 'wonderful you'. What is 'wonderful you' wearing? How is 'wonderful you' standing or moving? What sort of look does 'wonderful you' have on their face? Carry on until you feel admiration for 'wonderful you'. Again, take your time. There's no rush. Finally, give 'wonderful you' something to say that really encapsulates how you'd like to feel after having triumphed. It could be, 'I'm the master of this situation', or 'I never fail', or 'Easy!' or whatever you want.

Step 4: Take the image of 'wonderful you' and compress it into a sparkling dot. Place the dot into a blank screen and then let it grow and grow until it fills the screen. Hear 'wonderful you' speaking the words you decided in Step 3. Repeat this step over and over until you can reliably conjure up the sparkling dot and expand it. This is the hardest step in the visualization for most people and you may have to practise it for a while.

Step 5: Place the sparkling dot into the centre of the cue image from Step 1 and *Swish*. Make that bothersome cue image fade and disintegrate while the sparkling dot gets bigger and brighter and clearer. Inside that sparkling dot is 'wonderful you' successfully resisting the impulse and speaking the words from Step 3.

Step 6: Create a break by having a completely blank screen appear.

Step 7: Repeat Steps 4 to 6, getting faster and faster. It's impossible to say how many times will be necessary. Some people find two or three times are enough, others need ten and still others, 20.

Step 8: Try to recall the original cue image. If you can't, or if you can only do so with a struggle, then the process has worked. Never again let that negative cue image cloud your belief in yourself. Now go and test your new attitude in the real world.

Insight

This is a particularly difficult visualization. If you're having problems, I've found that thinking of photographs can be a better way to begin than by trying to recall the people or events themselves. And when it comes to visualizing *yourself*, photographs and home movies are better than trying to remember what you saw in the mirror. If you have difficulty manipulating that 'sparkling dot', instead try swapping over (Swishing) the image you want in place of the image you don't want, that is, the cue image you created in Step 1.

THE NEW BEHAVIOUR GENERATOR

You can use the New Behaviour Generator to translate an improving Big Five score into a whole scenario. It can be short and simple or you can make it as long and detailed as you like. You can test alternative moves, rehearse the one you like until it's perfect and then install it as a permanent behaviour. You're a star in your own movie.

Step 1: Identify the new behaviour you would like to have. For this example, let's say you want to be more expansive and charismatic (high Extroversion).

Step 2: You are the director of a movie in which you are also the star. As the director, give instructions to yourself about the way you should behave. Watch yourself exhibit the new behaviour. In your role as director, make any corrections or changes you think necessary.

Step 3: Once you're satisfied, step into the movie and experience what it's like to have this new way of behaving, as seen through your own eyes as the star. Not only see but, of course, hear everything and feel what it's like. Note the reaction of other people. Is it what you want it to be? Also check that this new behaviour really is suitable for you.

Step 4: If you're not happy with anything, return to your role as director, make the necessary changes and repeat Step 3.

Step 5: Visualize a situation in the future where you will want to behave in this new way – what's known in NLP as 'future pacing'. Look for a cue that could be used to trigger the behaviour automatically. For example, it might be the door to your boss's office, the door to a friend's apartment or, perhaps, the stage door at a theatre. Imagine yourself seeing or hearing the cue and immediately adopting the new behaviour. Play this 'film' as often as necessary until the new behaviour feels natural.

Step 6: Use the new behaviour in a real situation.

Making a real film
Not everybody can visualize well enough to make the New Behaviour Generator work as well as they'd like. If you find you're having problems, you could take on the roles of director and actor for real.

Step 1: Get hold of a DVD version of a film in which you've seen the type of behaviour you'd like to copy. Find a segment in which your character exhibits the behaviour and watch it several times.

Step 2: Get hold of a video camera of some sort. If you're completely uninhibited, you can ask someone to film you. Otherwise, set it up on a tripod – it will be a great help if you have the ability to connect it to your TV, which will then become a monitor. If you can't set up a monitor, then you'll have to get by as best you can. (Without a monitor, you may find that on your first attempt you've cut half of your head off or something like that. Never mind. Just make the necessary adjustments and try again.)

Step 3: Rehearse the behaviour then set the camera rolling.

Step 4: Watch the 'rushes'.

Step 5: Keep filming and watching and filming and watching until you think you've got the result you want. If necessary, inspire yourself by watching the original film again.

Step 6: Try out the new behaviour for real.

Getting motivated

NLP makes a distinction between two different kinds of motivation:

▶ motivation *away* from something
▶ motivation *towards* something.

Let's suppose you grew up in financially difficult circumstances. You knew what it was like to be hungry, you knew what it was like to be cold and you knew what it was like to wear the same clothes day after day, week after week. Now that you're an adult, you have a burning desire to be wealthy because you don't ever want to experience that kind of poverty again. That's motivation *away* from something.

Now let's suppose you're someone who grew up in an affluent family and have a well-paid job. But you still want to achieve more in the material sense. You dream of ocean-going yachts, private planes, heli-skiing in the winter, the Mediterranean in summer and so on. That's motivation *towards* something.

Of course, motivation direction doesn't have to be concerned with money. You can be motivated *away* from discomfort, confrontation, criticism, fear, pain, embarrassment, failure and so on, just as you can be motivated *towards* comfort, tranquillity, praise, success and much more.

Nobody is wholly 'away from' or 'towards' but, for any given type of situation, we all have a tendency to be mostly one or the other. In order to motivate yourself effectively, it helps to understand your own personality in this respect.

Think about the following and ask yourself whether your motivation is more 'away from' or more 'towards':

▶ studying
▶ going to work
▶ watching television
▶ meeting friends
▶ reading
▶ making love.

STOKING UP MOTIVATION

Having decided what kind of motivation works best with you, you can then stoke it up.

Suppose that, for various reasons, you wish to give up something – let's say, gambling. You've tried and you've failed. And the reason is this: you're motivated to stop gambling but your motivation to continue gambling is even stronger. Let's suppose you're an 'away from' person. What you have to do is stoke up your motivation *not* to gamble, until it overwhelms your motivation *to* gamble. In other words, to get you to the point at which you say 'enough is enough'. This is how to bring on that feeling through visualization.

Step 1: Think of five negative scenes connected with gambling (or whatever it might be). You could, for example, visualize the arrival of household bills you can't pay because you've lost money. You might think of how upset your partner is. You might think of the toll the stress is taking on your health. And so on.

Step 2: Run the five scenes in your mind one after the other to make your own 'anti-gambling' film. Then run them all again but faster. Then again, faster still. Continue until you have the overwhelming feeling 'enough is enough'.

Insight

If you're a 'towards' person, you would use the same procedure but by stacking five images of how wonderful it is to be a non-gambler.

BORROWING MOTIVATION

We all have things we need to do for which we can't get any motivation at all, either 'away from' or 'towards'.

NLP can help by, as it were, letting you borrow motivation from something you *do* enjoy. The following visualization utilizes the 'Swish' technique that you're now familiar with.

Step 1: Think of something you enjoy immensely and for which you feel tremendous motivation – for example, a romantic evening with your lover (Image 1). Make a note of the submodalities (that's to say, the qualities of the images, sounds and textures) associated with that motivational drive.

Step 2: Think of the thing you've got to do but for which you feel no motivation – for example, housework (Image 2).

Step 3: Enjoy Image 1. See, feel, touch, taste and smell everything associated with it. Spin it up as much as possible. Just when everything is at a peak, suddenly Swish Image 2 into the position occupied by Image 1. Maintain the submodalities from Image 1. Revel in your new, highly motivated attitude to this thing for which you previously felt no motivation at all. Repeat the Swish several times until you just can't wait to start on Image 2 for real.

Step 4: Go do it.

....
Insight
You may be able to bolster your motivation further by thinking of ways that dealing with one thing could actually *lead* to the other. For example, getting the housework done and the bedroom clean and tidy (Image 2) might really lead to a romantic evening (Image 1).
....

Anchoring a behaviour

The more you practise the various techniques, the more profound the change in your personality will be. Even so, it's going to take time and there are going to be occasions when, under physical or mental stress, you're still likely to react in the old way. Wouldn't it be useful if you could actually program yourself so the desired response was more assured?

NLP has a technique known as 'anchoring', which Bandler and Grinder explain as 'the tendency for any one element of an experience to bring back the entire experience'.

If you're driving a car and you see brake lights go on ahead of you, without even thinking, you take your foot off the accelerator and move it to the brake pedal. In this example, brake lights are the anchor (or trigger) and the action of braking is a programmed response. Notice, however, that the anchor doesn't actually *compel* you to brake – you retain your freedom to perform a different action if you judge that the situation demands it. That's the principle we're going to use to make your desired behaviours more secure.

Insight

Think back to the things you do before facing various sorts of demanding situations. Are there, perhaps, little rituals you perform that, in reality, have no practical benefit but make you feel 'right'? These are 'anchors'. Make a list of them. Later, using the technique below, you can learn to amplify them.

CHOOSING ANCHORS

Ideally, an anchor should meet the following conditions:

▶ It has genuine meaning or intrinsic connection with the desired emotion, belief or action (in the case of the 'brake light anchor' we know it only comes on when the driver in front presses his brake pedal and slows down).

▶ You *want* to respond to the anchor (otherwise you'll collide with the car in front).

▶ It should be easy to activate, but not to activate accidentally (everyone can press a brake pedal).

▶ You're fully capable of responding to the anchor (again, everyone can press a brake pedal).

▶ It should combine two or preferably three senses (the brake light anchor fails on this – the addition of an audible signal would be an improvement).

Let's say you'd like to be higher in Agreeableness. You've used some of the techniques above but you keep getting caught out when people say things you disagree with. You find it hard to hold back and consider their ideas with the respect they deserve. Other people find you irritable and, quite frankly, disagreeable. What you need to do is anchor a feeling of patience so you don't snap at them without thinking things through. Of course, you can adapt this procedure for anything you want.

Step 1: Choose your anchors. For patience I'm going to suggest you stroke your chin, which involves the optimum three senses. It's:

▶ A visual anchor: the sight of your hand coming up to your chin and moving in front of your chin.

▶ An audible anchor: the sound of your fingers against the skin of your face; behind the concealment of your hand you could also whisper the word 'patience'.

▶ A kinaesthetic anchor: the feeling of your fingers against the skin of your face.

Step 2: Think of a time when you felt truly serene, calm, imperturbable and, above all, patient. However, if you really can't recall such a time, then imagine the feeling or recall a film in which someone you admire exhibited supreme patience.

Step 3: Revel in that feeling of patience. See, hear, touch, taste and smell everything to do with that patience.

Step 4: Just *before* your feeling of patience reaches its peak, set your anchors by gently stroking your chin and whispering the word 'patience'. Repeat the process several times.

Step 5: Visualize a scene that demands patience and watch yourself responding with patience.

Step 6: As soon as possible, deliberately seek out a situation that will test your patience a little. Fire your anchors. Over the next few days, keep on experiencing irritating situations and keep on firing your anchors. You will need to deal successfully with maybe a score of situations before the anchor will start to become reliable.

Insight

The setting of anchors can be quite an art.

As I emphasized in Step 4, you need to do it just *before* the emotion you're dealing with reaches peak intensity. In that way, the anchor will be associated with strong and growing emotion. If you set your anchor *after* peak emotion, then it will be associated with a decline in feeling, which is not the result you want at all.

The anchor also needs to be pure. In other words, if you're, say, feeling sceptical when you try this procedure, then you'll be anchoring patience contaminated with scepticism – again, not the result you want.

Self-hypnosis

Self-hypnosis is an extremely powerful tool. There are various
methods but the one I'm going to describe here is both simple and
effective. It's attributed to Betty Erickson, wife of the most famous
hypnotist of the era, Milton H. Erickson (1901–80), and herself a
hypnotherapist.

But, first of all, we should perhaps try to establish exactly what
hypnotism is. Don't expect to be able to float above the ground rigid
as a board. That sort of thing is stage magic. The hypnotic state
is simply an altered state of consciousness or, more specifically, a
state of consciousness that's different to what we consider to be our
normal waking state.

In other words, it's a trance. In fact, we all go into trances every day.
When you're totally absorbed in a book or a newspaper and unaware
of the things going on around you, you're in a trance. It's as simple
as that. When you swing a golf club or throw a dart and get almost
exactly the result you want, you're in a trance. When you're making
love with your partner, you're in a trance.

Once you've learned to put yourself into a trance using this
technique, you'll be able to bring about significant changes to your
personality – I've used it successfully for all kinds of things. It's
essential, therefore, that you're quite sure you want to make the
changes and that people around you will also be happy. So be sure
to carry out the NLP ecology check as described in the previous
chapter.

Have a go

Step 1: Get yourself comfortable in a place you won't be disturbed. It's not a good idea to lie on the bed because you might fall asleep. But you could sit up on the bed supported by pillows, or arrange yourself in a nice, comfy chair.

Step 2: Decide the length of time you wish to spend in self-hypnosis. Initially I'd suggest ten minutes. That should give you enough time to achieve a deep state of trance without feeling anxiety about 'wasting' time or needing to get on with something else. As you get used to self-hypnosis, you can increase the time. So, having got comfortable, you should say something like this: 'I am now going to hypnotize myself for ten minutes.' You might like to append the actual time by adding '...which means I will come out of self-hypnosis at 19.30' (or whatever).

Step 3: This is a key step because it's where you state the purpose of your hypnosis. During your initial experiments, I'd suggest starting with one of the more minor changes to your personality, leaving your biggest issues to be dealt with once you've become proficient in the technique. The exact words aren't important. Something along these lines will do fine. 'I am entering into a state of self-hypnosis so that I can hand over to my unconscious mind the task of...' Or: 'I am entering into a trance for the purpose of allowing my unconscious mind to make the adjustments that will help me to...' For example, you might add 'feel more confident' or 'feel more sociable' or 'be more empathetic to others'. Whatever you say, make sure it includes the message that you are inviting your *unconscious* to deal with the matter.

Step 4: State how you want to feel when you come out of your trance. It may be you will simply want to experience your 'normal waking state'. It might be you will immediately want to make use of the change your unconscious has made. In that case you might say, for example, '...and as I come out of my trance I will feel full of confidence' (or full of love for other people, or whatever). Or it may be that you simply want to continue feeling relaxed or even go to sleep.

Step 5: This is the actual process of self-hypnosis. Basically you're going to engage your three main representational systems in turn to bring the trance about; in other words, your visual system or sight, your auditory system or hearing, and your kinaesthetic system or sense of touch. So in the first part of the process you will be noting things you can actually see, hear and feel *in the room where you are*. In the second part you will be noting things you can see, hear and feel *in an imaginary scene*.

Below is a diagram that represents the whole process. In the diagram, V = Visual system, A = Auditory system, and K = Kinaesthetic system.

```
        V           V           V
        A           A           A
        K           K           K
                V           V
                A           A
                K           K
                        V
                        A
                        K
```

(External)
- -
(Internal)

```
                        V
                        A
                        K
                V           V
                A           A
                K           K
        V           V           V
        A           A           A
        K           K           K
```

In this process, some people talk to themselves internally but I recommend that *you say everything out loud*. For that reason you'll want to be in a private place. You might imagine that you'd 'wake' yourself up but, in fact, the sound of your own voice, done the right way, will intensify the effect. (If, however, speaking out loud doesn't work for you, then, by all means, speak internally.)

Step 5a: From your comfortable position look at some small thing in the room in front of you and say out loud what you are looking at. Choose things you can see without moving your head. For example, 'I am looking at the door handle.' Then, without rushing, focus on another small item. For example, 'I am now looking at a glass of water on the table.' Then move on to a third item. For example, 'I am looking at the light switch.' When you have your three visual references, move on to Step 5b.

Step 5b: Switch attention to sounds and, in the same way, note one after another until you have three, each time saying out loud what you're hearing. Then move on to Step 5c.

Step 5c: Note things that you can feel with your body. For example, you might say, 'I can feel the seat pressing against my buttocks.' When you have your three, move on.

Step 5d: Now repeat steps 5a to 5c, but with only two items for each sense, that's to say, two images, two sounds and two feelings. They must be *different* from the ones you used before. *Speak a little more slowly*.

Step 5e: Again repeat steps 5a to 5c but with only one item per sense, that's to say, one image, one sound and one feeling. Again, they must be *different* from any that have gone before. *Speak even more slowly*.

Step 5f: Close your eyes, if they're not already closed, and think of a scene. Any scene will do. It could be the first thing that comes into your head. But the effect will be more powerful if the scene is relevant to what you're trying to achieve. For example, if you're trying to feel more sociable and more loving towards other people, then you might imagine a scene in which you're surrounded by friends and family, deeply enjoying their company. Using visualization in this way, while under self-hypnosis, will increase the effect.

Step 5g: Using this imagined scene, go through the same process you already used for the real scene, but beginning with just one example of each of the three senses, that is, one image, one sound and one feeling. Don't forget that the image will be just one tiny thing within your fantasy scene, not the entire scene. When you've done that, increase to two examples and then three. (Three is usually enough, but if you've stipulated a lengthy session you may need to continue with your fantasy scene by going on to name four images, sounds and feelings, or five or even more.) Remember, each example must be *different*. You'll probably find you're automatically speaking very slowly now but, if not, make a point of *slowing your voice down more and more*.

Step 5h: After the allotted time you should begin to come out of trance automatically. But it may help to announce, 'I'll count to three and when I reach three I'll be (whatever you said in Step 4).' Don't worry about getting 'stuck' in a trance. That won't happen. You may feel a little woozy for a while. If so, don't drive a car or do anything demanding until you're sure you're okay to do so.

Insight

This method works by causing your unconscious to deal with the stated purpose of your self-hypnosis all the time you're in trance and, possibly, afterwards too. Of course, if you'd gone to see a hypnotist he or she would have continued to speak to you in trance for a stronger effect. One session might be all that's necessary but the effect will probably wear off over time. To ensure a more permanent change, give yourself several sessions over a month and the occasional booster session thereafter.

If you'd like to take it further, you'll find full details in my book, *Transform Your Life with NLP* (see Taking it further).

10 TIPS FOR SUCCESS

1 Visualizations can be used to change your personality.

2 Cinematic techniques will increase the power of your visualizations.

3 Changing the submodalities (qualities) of images, sounds and textures will change the way you feel.

4 The Magic Circle is a technique for enveloping yourself in your new personality.

5 Swishing is a way of 'borrowing' emotion.

6 You can use the New Behaviour Generator to try out a new personality.

7 If you have a problem with visualization, then make a real film of yourself.

8 Some people are motivated *towards* things, others *away from* things.

9 Anchoring is a way of making a new behaviour more assured.

10 Self-hypnosis is an easy and powerful technique for making profound changes.

Taking it further

First of all I'd like to invite you to take a look at my website
www.pauljenner.eu. I'm constantly adding material related to my
books and I'd certainly welcome your comments and contributions to
any of the ongoing topics.

If you've enjoyed this book, you might be interested in some of my
others:

Beat Your Depression (Hodder Arnold, 2007)

From the Teach Yourself series:

How To Be Happier (Hodder Education, 2010)

Transform Your Life With NLP (Hodder Education, 2010)

Be More Confident (Hodder Education, 2010)

Have Great Sex (Hodder Education, 2010)

Get Intimate With Tantric Sex (Hodder Education, 2010)

Help Yourself To Live Longer (Hodder Education, 2010)

From the Bullet Guide series:

Beat Negativity With CBT (Hodder Education, 2011)

Several of these titles are available in abridged form in the Flash
series:

Life-Changing Happiness

Amazing Sex the Tantric Way

Kickstart Your Life With NLP

Master the Art of Confidence

OTHER BOOKS

Andreas, S. and Faulkner, C., *NLP – The New Technology Of
Achievement* (Nicholas Brealey, 1996).

This is very much about finding your role in life and achieving your
goals, with an emphasis on NLP visualization techniques.

Argyle, M., *The Psychology Of Happiness* (Routledge, 1987).

Bandler, R. and Grinder, J., *Frogs Into Princes* (Real People Press, 1979).

This is the book that really popularized Neuro-Linguistic Programming (NLP) and is actually the transcript of a live training session.

Bandler, R. and Grinder, J., *The Structure of Magic,* Volumes 1 & 2 (Meta Publications, 1975).

The very first books from the Bandler/Grinder team, these two volumes are mainly of interest to therapists.

Bavister, S. and Vickers, A., *Teach Yourself NLP* (Hodder Education, 2008).

A comprehensive and very readable description of everything in NLP by two certified NLP coaches. A good book for anyone going on an NLP course.

Broks, P., *Into The Silent Land* (Atlantic Books, 2003).

Elegant but ultimately frightening account of the way illness and brain damage can destroy personality.

Burns, D. D., *Feeling Good – The New Mood Therapy* (Avon Books, 1999).

An excellent introduction to cognitive therapy (CT) and how to use it for self-help.

Dawkins, R., *The Selfish Gene* (Oxford, 1976).

Explanation of how genes work.

Diener, E. and Biswas Diener, R., *Happiness: Unlocking The Mysteries Of Psychological Wealth* (Wiley Blackwell, 2008).

Edwards, B., *Drawing On The Right Side Of The Brain* (Harper Collins, 2001).

A course for enhancing creativity.

Erickson, M. H., and Rossi, E. L., *Hypnotherapy – An Explanatory Casebook* (Irvington, 1979).

This is a much more readable account of Erickson's methods than Bandler and Grinder's *Patterns of the Hypnotic Techniques of Milton H Erickson*. Rossi describes Erickson's techniques in plain language and includes transcripts of Erickson's actual words together with explanatory comments.

Gilbert, D., *Stumbling On Happiness* (HarperCollins, 2006).

You'll find happiness by chance if you give yourself enough opportunities.

Goleman, D., *Emotional Intelligence* (Bloomsbury, 1996).

An examination of the aspects of human personality concerned with sociability and relationships.

Gray, J., *Men Are From Mars, Women Are From Venus* (Element, 2002).

It may have been hugely popular but that doesn't mean it can't be good, too.

Klein, S., *The Science Of Happiness* (Marlowe & Company, 2002).

Layard, R., *Happiness: Lessons From A New Science* (Penguin, 2006).

Nettle, D., *Happiness: The Science Behind Your Smile* (OUP, 2006).

Nettle, D., *Personality* (Oxford, 2007).

Highly readable explanation of the Big Five.

Pinker, S., *How The Mind Works* (Penguin, 1997).

Engaging in-depth look at perception, memory, consciousness and all the other puzzles of the mind.

Pinker, S., *The Blank Slate* (Penguin, 2002).

Compelling argument that differences in personality are about 50 per cent due to genes.

Tannen, D., *You Just Don't Understand* (Virago Press, 1991).

Why men and women use language differently and what they really mean.

Walsh, A., *The Science of Love* (Prometheus Books, 1996).

Worth reading again and again for its insights into the most important human relationships.

Wiseman, R., *Paranormality* (Macmillan, 2001).

If you're excited by the supernatural, you'll be sorry you ever read this.

Wright, L., *Twins* (Weidenfeld & Nicolson, 1997).

Fascinating insight into the world of twins and what they can tell us about identity.

WEBSITES

http://authentichappiness.org

Website of Dr Martin Seligman, founder of 'Positive Psychology'.

www.Bradburyac.mistral.co.uk

Run by Andy Bradbury, author of *Develop Your NLP Skills*, this site includes articles, reviews, frequently asked questions and useful links.

www.forgivenessproject.com

Advice on how to forgive.

www.mheap.com/nlp.html

Michael Heap, a clinical and forensic psychologist, takes issue with some of the claims for NLP.

www.nlpu.com

Masses of material here by Robert Dilts, a leading figure in NLP, as well as the Encyclopedia of NLP, which explains all that jargon.

www.positivepsychology.org

Website of the 'Positive Psychology' movement.

http://pursuit-of-happiness.org

How to pursue happiness through education.

www.stefanklein.info

Website of Stefan Klein, author of *The Science of Happiness*.

www.stressinstitute.com

Tips on how to avoid stress and how to cope with it.

www.stumblingonhappiness.com

Website of Daniel Gilbert who wrote *Stumbling On Happiness*.

http://worlddatabaseofhappiness.eur.nl

Data on various aspects of happiness all over the world.

NLP COACHING

If you're interested in going further with Neuro-Linguistic Programming (NLP) as featured in Chapter 13, there are NLP coaches all over the world, specializing in all kinds of things. If you would like to find an NLP practitioner near you, you may find the following websites useful:

www.anlp.org

The website of the UK-based Association for Neuro-Linguistic Programming, with a searchable database of practitioners.

www.bbnlp.com

Website of the British Board of NLP with a searchable database.

www.nlpschedule.com

Includes a database of NLP practitioners in the UK.

www.nlptca.com

The website of the Neuro Linguistic Psychotherapy and Counselling Association in the UK, with a searchable directory of members.

It's important to check what kind of training and experience an NLP practitioner has. Standards can vary enormously. Have a chat on the phone and don't commit yourself to anything beyond the preliminary session so you'll have the chance to make up your mind based on how that goes.

If you would actually like to train to become an NLP coach, you may find the following websites of interest:

www.inlpta.co.uk

Website for the International NLP Trainers Association, which has members in over 20 countries.

www.johngrinder.co.uk

John Grinder is the co-founder of NLP and here you'll find details of his seminars in the UK.

www.johngrinder.com

Details of New Code NLP which was developed by John Grinder and others after he and Richard Bandler went their separate ways.

www.nlp.org

A seminar searcher.

www.ppdlearning.co.uk

Provides various courses for NLP professionals including 21 days to become a practitioner – lecturers include leading names in NLP such as Robert Dilts, Joseph O'Connor, Judith DeLozier and Charles Faulkner.

www.professionalguildofnlp.com

Website of the Professional Guild of NLP that provides details of training courses available.

www.richardbandler.com

Website of the co-creator of NLP.

Training courses vary considerably. It's attractive to think that you can help other people on the basis of a single weekend course but, realistically, you need to think in terms of something much longer. Online courses can seem a good idea but be careful you're not paying a large sum of money for information you could have obtained much more cheaply from books. When it comes to working with clients, there's no substitute for practical training.

Index